# STAND OUT

## Evidence-Based Learning for College and Career Readiness

**3**

THIRD EDITION

## WORKBOOK

### STACI JOHNSON

### ROB JENKINS

Australia • Brazil • Mexico • Singapore • United Kingdom • United States

**Stand Out 3: Evidence-Based Learning
for College and Career Readiness,
Third Edition
Staci Johnson and Rob Jenkins
Workbook**

Publisher: Sherrise Roehr

Executive Editor: Sarah Kenney

Development Editor: Lewis Thompson

Assistant Editor: Patricia Giunta

Director of Global Marketing: Ian Martin

Executive Marketing Manager: Ben Rivera

Product Marketing Manager: Dalia Bravo

Media Researcher: Leila Hishmeh

Director of Content and Media Production:
    Michael Burggren

Production Manager: Daisy Sosa

Senior Print Buyer: Mary Beth Hennebury

Cover and Interior Designer:
    Brenda Carmichael

Composition: Lumina

Cover Image: Hero Images/Getty Images

Bottom Images: (Left to Right) Jay B Sauceda/
    Getty Images; Tripod/Getty Images; Portra
    Images/Getty Images; Portra Images/Getty
    Images; Mark Edward Atkinson/Tracey Lee/
    Getty Images; James Porter/Getty Images;
    Jade/Getty Images; Seth Joel/Getty Images;
    LWA/Larry Williams/Getty Images; Dimitri
    Otis/Getty Images

For permission to use material from this text or product,
submit all requests online at **cengage.com/permissions**
Further permissions questions can be emailed to
**permissionrequest@cengage.com**

Work Book
ISBN 13: 978-1-305-65554-6

**National Geographic Learning/Cengage Learning**
20 Channel Center Street
Boston, MA 02210
USA

Cengage Learning is a leading provider of customized learning solutions
with office locations around the globe, including Singapore, the United Kingdom,
Australia, Mexico, Brazil and Japan. Locate our local office at:
**www.cengage.com/global**

Cengage Learning products are represented in Canada by Nelson Education, Ltd.

Visit National Geographic Learning online at **NGL.Cengage.com**
Visit our corporate website at **www.cengage.com**

Printed in the United States of America
Print Number: 07     Print Year: 2020

# CONTENTS

# TO THE TEACHER

## ABOUT THE SERIES

The **Stand Out** series is designed to facilitate *active* learning within life-skill settings that leads students to career and academic pathways. Each student book and its supplemental components in the six-level series expose students to competency areas most useful and essential for newcomers, with careful treatment of level-appropriate but challenging materials. Students grow academically by developing essential literacy and critical thinking skills that will help them find personal success in a changing and dynamic world.

## STAND OUT WORKBOOK

The **Stand Out Workbook** is designed to provide additional practice for learners to reinforce what they learned in each student book lesson. It can be used as homework or as a supplement to the lesson in the classroom. Each lesson in **Stand Out** is driven by a life-skill objective and supported by vocabulary and grammar. Students are not expected to master or acquire vocabulary and grammar completely after being exposed to it just one time, hence the need for additional practice. The lessons in the student book are three pages long and each supporting workbook lesson is also three pages long. The workbook lessons correlate directly with the student book lessons.

The **Stand Out Workbook** establishes a link to new content by providing the essential vocabulary introduced in the books in a way that also promotes critical thinking skills. Promoting critical thinking skills is essential for students to become independent lifelong learners. About half of the three-page practice is grammar focused where students are given a chart with notes, study how the grammar facilitates communication, and gain additional needed confidence through practice.

## HOW TO USE THE STAND OUT WORKBOOK

The workbook can be used in the following ways:

1. The activities in the workbook can be used as additional practice during class to reinforce one or more practice activities in the student book.

2. The activities in the workbook can be assigned as homework. This is often a good way to reinforce what students have learned. The skills, vocabulary, and structures may not transfer into long-term memory after the lesson, so reinforcing the lesson after a short period of time away can be very helpful. Additionally, teachers can also review the homework at the beginning of each class, giving students another opportunity to be exposed to the information. Reviewing the homework is also a good strategy for the *Warm-up/Review* portion of the lesson and can be used in place of the one proposed in the **Stand Out Lesson Planner**.

3. The **Stand Out Workbook** can be used as a tool in the flipped classroom. In flipped classrooms, students prepare for lessons away from class before they are presented. Since the **Stand Out Workbook** introduces much of the vocabulary and grammar for each lesson, it is ideal for incorporating this approach.

## ADDITIONAL PRACTICE

The **Stand Out** series is a comprehensive one-stop for all student needs. There is no need to look any further than the resources offered. Additional practice is available through the online workbook, which is different from the print workbook. There are also hundreds of multi-level worksheets available online. Please visit ngl.cengage.com/so3 to get easy access to all resources.

# LESSON **1** Nice to meet you!

**GOAL** ■ Introduce yourself and greet others

## A. How do you greet people? Read the following conversations.

**Miguel:** Hi Janie. How's it going?

**Janie:** Pretty good. I really like my ESL class. What's new?

**Miguel:** Not much. I still have to register for class.

**Janie:** Well, I hope you're in my class. You'll really like the teacher.

**Miguel:** Sounds good. I'll see you around.

**Janie:** Bye.


**Binh:** Hey Sara. What's up?

**Sara:** Not much. I'm just doing my homework.

**Binh:** Homework on the first day of school? Wow!

**Sara:** It's pretty easy so far. What's new?

**Binh:** I start a new job today, so I'm really excited.

**Sara:** That's great! I hope you'll still have time for school.

**Binh:** Yeah, me too!

## B. Look at the greetings and responses below.

| Greetings | Responses |
|---|---|
| What's up?<br>What's going on?<br>What's happening?<br>What's new? | Not much.<br>Nothing. |
| How's it going?<br>How are you?<br>How are things? | Good.<br>Pretty good.<br>Not bad.<br>Not so good.<br>Bad. |

**C.** A contraction is when two words are combined with an apostrophe ('). Underline all of the contractions in the two conversations in Exercise A.

**D.** Study the contractions you may hear when people talk.

| Contractions in Greetings | |
|---|---|
| **Expression** | **Contraction** |
| How's it going? | *How's* = How is |
| What's up? | |
| What's new? | |
| What's happening? | *What's* = What is |
| What's going on? | |

| Verb *Be* | Contraction |
|---|---|
| I am | I'm |
| You are | You're |
| He is | He's |
| She is | She's |
| We are | We're |
| They are | They're |

**E.** Underline the contraction in each expression. Then write the words on the lines.

1. <u>What's</u> up? _____ *What is* _____

2. They're doing well. _____

3. I'm great! _____

4. How's it going? _____

5. It's going really well. _____

6. What's up? _____

7. He's got class in the morning. _____

8. She's working. _____

**F.** **Underline the two words in each sentence that can be combined to make a contraction. Rewrite the sentence using the contraction.**

1. <u>How is</u> your new class? *How's your new class?* _____

2. What is up with you? _____

3. I will see you later. _____

4. What is happening? _____

5. That is wonderful! _____

6. How is your family doing? _____

**G.** **Fill out the application below.**

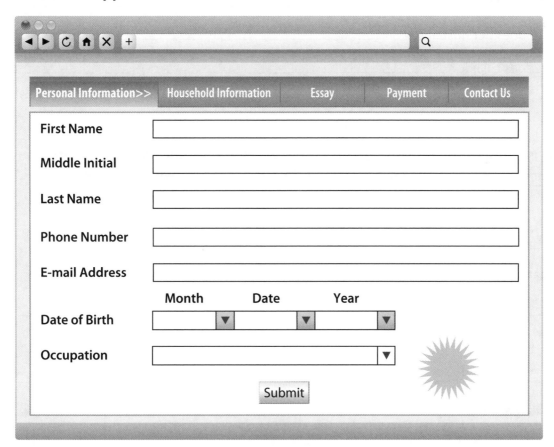

**H.** **Write a question that somebody may ask you based on the application. Remember to use a contraction.**

_____

**GOAL** ■ Write about yourself

**A. Read Lilia's story.**

> My name is Lilia Alvarado. I'm a student at Orange Adult Learning Center. My husband and I live in Villa Park. He works in a machine shop and I go to school and take care of our children. We want to be successful in this country. My husband wants to own his own business one day, and I hope to become a teacher.

**B. Answer the questions about Lilia and her family.**

1. Where does Lilia live? _____

2. Where does her husband work? _____

3. What does Lilia do? _____

4. What does Lilia hope to do in the future? _____

**C. Below is some more information about Lilia and her family. Write complete sentences using this information. More than one answer can be correct.**

1. teach kindergarten

   Lilia wants to teach kindergarten.

2. study English

   _____

3. three children

   _____

4. Grant's Machines

   _____

5. all girls

   _____

**D.** Look again at Lilia's paragraph in Exercise A and underline all of the main present tense verbs. (Hint: The main verb always comes right after the subject.)

**Example:** My name is Lilia Alvarado.

subject     main verb

**E.** Study the charts.

| Present Tense | | | | | |
|---|---|---|---|---|---|
| **Subject** | **Rule** | **Present tense verbs** | | | |
| I, You, We, They | base verb* | work | live | want | hope |
| He, She, It | base verb + -s | works | lives | wants | hopes |
| I, You, We, They | base verb | go | watch | | |
| He, She, It | base verb + -es | goes | watches | | |
| *base verb = the pure verb form (to be: <u>be</u> = the base verb; to go: <u>go</u> = the base verb) | | | | | |

| Present Tense *Be* | |
|---|---|
| **Subject** | ***Be*** |
| I | am |
| You, We, They | are |
| He, She, It | is |

**F.** Choose the correct form of the verb. Check (✓) the correct answer.

1. Kimla _____ in Fountain Valley.   ☐ live   ☐ lives

2. I _____ to move into a bigger house.   ☐ want   ☐ wants

3. George _____ every morning before he comes to school.   ☐ work   ☐ works

4. We _____ to school together.   ☐ go   ☐ goes

5. She _____ to finish her high school diploma next year.   ☐ hope   ☐ hopes

6. They _____ near the bus stop.   ☐ live   ☐ lives

7. I _____ three English classes.   ☐ take   ☐ takes

8. Ellie _____ at the university.   ☐ study   ☐ studies

**G.** **Complete the paragraph with the correct present tense verb form.**

My name _____ (be) Jaime Kinaste. I _____ (attend) Long Beach School for Adults. I _____ (have) English class every weekday, and I _____ (work) every night. I _____ (be) a busboy at a local pizza restaurant. I _____ (want) to be a cashier, so I _____ (need) to study math. Someday, I _____ (hope) to get my high school diploma and _____ (go) to college.

**H.** **Answer the questions about yourself using present tense verbs.**

1. What is your name? _____

2. Where do you attend school? _____

3. When do you have English class? _____

4. When do you work? _____

5. What do you want to be? _____

**I.** **Using the information from the questions in Exercise H, write a paragraph about yourself.**

_____

_____

_____

_____

_____

_____

# LESSON **3** Are you college bound?

**GOAL** ■ Identify goals

**A.** Look at Matthew's educational timeline.

| Preschool | Elementary School | Junior High | High School | Community College |
|---|---|---|---|---|
| 2002–2004 | 2004–2010 | 2010–2012 | 2012–2016 | 2016– |

**B.** Answer the questions about Matthew.

1. When did Matthew go to preschool? _____

2. When did he finish elementary school? _____

3. When did he start junior high school? _____

4. How many years did he go to high school? _____

**C.** Fill in the steps on the educational pyramid.

| high school | ~~preschool~~ | college |
|---|---|---|
| elementary school | graduate school | vocational education |
| middle school | community college | kindergarten |

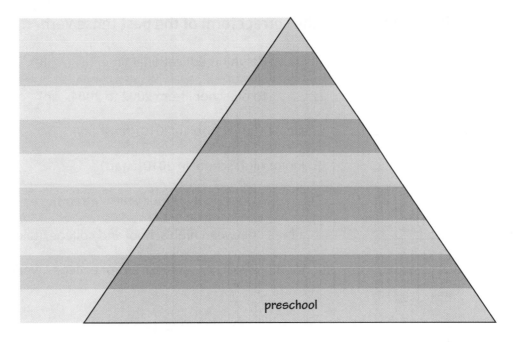

preschool

## D. Study the charts.

| Past Tense (Regular Verbs) | | | | |
|---|---|---|---|---|
| **Subject** | **Rule** | **Past tense verbs** | | |
| I, You, We, They<br>He, She, It | base verb + -*ed* | worked | started | wanted |
| | | finished | helped | attended |
| I, You, We, They<br>He, She, It | base verb + -*d* | lived | liked | |
| | | hoped | completed | |
| I, You, We, They<br>He, She, It | base verb –*y* + -*ied* | studied | hurried | married |
| | | worried | carried | |

| Past Tense (Irregular Verbs) | | |
|---|---|---|
| **Subject** | **Base form** | **Irregular form** |
| I, You, We, They<br>He, She, It | go | **went** |
| | take | **took** |
| | come | **came** |
| | have | **had** |
| *For a more complete list of irregular verbs, see pages 142–155. | | |

| Past Tense *Be* | |
|---|---|
| **Subject** | ***Be*** |
| I | **was** |
| You, We, They | **were** |
| He, She, It | **was** |

## E. Complete the sentences with the correct form of the past tense verb.

1. Matthew _____ *wrote* _____ down his educational timeline. (write)

2. Matthew _____ to preschool from 2002 to 2004. (go)

3. He _____ elementary school in 2010. (finish)

4. He _____ junior high school in 2010. (start)

5. Matthew _____ high school for four years. (attend)

6. He _____ a break between high school and college. (take)

7. He _____ for three years to save money for college. (work)

**F.** Complete your educational timeline. Write the schools you went to and the years you attended.

| School | | | | | |
|--------|--|--|--|--|--|
| Years | | | | | |

**G.** Write sentences about your educational history using the verbs in parentheses.

1. (start) _____

_____

2. (finish) _____

_____

3. (attend) _____

_____

4. (go) _____

_____

5. (take) _____

_____

6. (work) _____

_____

7. (study) _____

_____

8. (complete) _____

_____

# LESSON **1** Everyday life

**GOAL** ■ Analyze and create schedules

**A.** Look at the frequency adverbs. Put them in order from *always* to *never*. Then, write definitions.

| ~~always~~ | ~~never~~ | often | sometimes | rarely | usually |
|---|---|---|---|---|---|

1. __always__ . all the time _____

2. _____ : _____

3. _____ : _____

4. _____ : _____

5. _____ : _____

6. __never__ : _____

**B.** Look at Julio's schedule and make sentences using the frequency adverbs from Exercise A.

| | Mon | Tues | Wed | Thurs | Fri | Sat | Sun |
|---|---|---|---|---|---|---|---|
| **7 a.m.** | bike ride | bike ride | bike ride | bike ride | bike ride | bike ride | bike ride |
| **8 a.m.** | work | volunteer | work | volunteer | work | work | work |
| **10 a.m.** | work | volunteer | work | volunteer | work | work | work |
| **12 p.m.** | work | lunch | work | lunch | work | work | work |
| **2 p.m.** | work | study | work | study | work | work | work |
| **4 p.m.** | work | study | work | study | work | work | work |
| **6 p.m.** | dinner | dinner | dinner | dinner | dinner | dinner | dinner |
| **8 p.m.** | ESL Class | ESL Class | ESL Class | ESL Class | see friends | see friends | visit family |

1. _____

2. _____

3. _____

4. _____

5. _____

6. _____

**C. Look again at Julio's schedule. Answer the questions on a separate piece of paper.**

1. When does Julio exercise?
2. How many days a week does Julio work?
3. At what time does Julio go to ESL class?
4. How often does Julio eat dinner?
5. What does Julio do once a week?
6. How often does Julio volunteer?

**D. Study the chart.**

| Adverbs of Frequency | | | |
|---|---|---|---|
| **Adverb** | **Frequency** | **Example** | **Rule** |
| always | 100% | Julio **always** rides his bike in the morning. | Frequency adverbs come before the main verb but after the verb *Be*. |
| usually | | Julio **usually** works from 8 a.m.– until 6 p.m. **Usually**, Julio works from 8 a.m.– until 6 p.m. | |
| often | | Julio **often** has ESL class at night. **Often**, Julio has ESL class at night. | |
| sometimes | | **Sometimes**, Julio visits his family. Julio **sometimes** visits his family. | |
| rarely/seldom | | Julio is **seldom** at home. | |
| never | 0% | Julio **never** has free time. | |

**E. Choose the correct frequency adverb. Check (✓) the correct answer.**

1. I am never late to school. I am _____ on time.  ☐ seldom  ☐ always

2. I usually study at the library. I _____ study at home.  ☐ often  ☐ rarely

3. Every Saturday and Sunday, I sleep late. I _____ sleep late on weekends.  ☐ never  ☐ always

4. Michel seldom has time to study. He _____ needs more time.  ☐ always  ☐ never

5. Luisa goes to school every day. She _____ misses class.  ☐ seldom  ☐ usually

6. We always try to be quiet. We _____ disturb others.  ☐ often  ☐ rarely

7. They try to go for a walk once a day. They _____ exercise.  ☐ never  ☐ usually

**F.** **Rewrite the sentences with frequency adverbs.**

1. he accomplishes everything that needs to get done (usually)

   <u>He usually *accomplishes everything that needs to get done.*</u>

2. they are very busy in the morning (always)

   _____

3. she finds time to relax (rarely)

   _____

4. we make time for our family (often)

   _____

5. he eats lunch in the office (sometimes)

   _____

6. I get a chance to take a break (never)

   _____

7. Erica finds time to exercise after work (always)

   _____

**G.** **Complete the schedule. Then, write three sentences about your schedule using frequency adverbs.**

|           | Mon | Tues | Wed | Thurs | Fri | Sat | Sun |
|-----------|-----|------|-----|-------|-----|-----|-----|
| morning   |     |      |     |       |     |     |     |
| afternoon |     |      |     |       |     |     |     |
| evening   |     |      |     |       |     |     |     |

1. _____

2. _____

3. _____

# L E S S O N ② Goals, obstacles, and solutions

**GOAL** ■ Identify goals and obstacles and suggest solutions

## A. Match.

| | |
|---|---|
| 1. goal | a. problem |
| 2. political prisoner | b. money needed to maintain a certain level of living |
| 3. solution | c. a way to solve a problem |
| 4. living expenses | d. money given to a student based on academic or other achievement |
| 5. obstacle | e. something you would like to achieve in the future |
| 6. scholarship | f. a person imprisoned for their political beliefs or actions |

## B. Read Lam's story.

Lam came to the United States from Vietnam many years ago. He was a political prisoner during the Vietnam War, and now he's happy to be safe in America with his family. His goal is to send his granddaughters to college. He wants them to have the education he never did, so he thinks it's important for them to go to school. But he doesn't have enough money, so he and the girls came up with a few solutions. When they apply to college, they will look for scholarships. This is a good idea because both girls are very smart. Also, when they go to school, they will get part-time jobs. Finally, when Lam has extra money, he will send the girls checks every month to help them with living expenses. Lam hopes everything will work out in the end.

## C. Answer the questions about Lam on a separate piece of paper.

1. Where is Lam from?
2. What is his goal?
3. What is his problem?
4. What are the three solutions to his problem?

## D. Look at the three solutions in Exercise B. Underline the verbs in those three sentences.

**E.  Study the chart.**

<table>
<tr><td colspan="2">Future Time Clauses with when</td></tr>
<tr><td>Time clause<br>(simple present)</td><td>Independent clause<br>(future tense with will)</td></tr>
<tr><td>When they apply to college,</td><td>they will look for scholarships.</td></tr>
<tr><td>When they go to school,</td><td>they will get part-time jobs.</td></tr>
<tr><td>When Lam has extra money,</td><td>he will send the girls checks to help them with living expenses.</td></tr>
<tr><td colspan="2">*Note: The order of the clauses does not matter. When they apply to college, they will look for scholarships. and They will look for scholarships when they apply to college. have the same meaning.</td></tr>
</table>

**F.  Correct the mistake in each sentence.**

1. When I ~~will~~ move to New York, I will buy a new house.
2. When they register for class, they bought their books.
3. Michael will get his real estate license, when he will pass the test.
4. When Susana gets settled, she sends for her family.
5. When Lam get some money, he will send it to his grandchildren.
6. Tuba will gets a job when her children are in school.

**G.  Use the words to write a sentences that begins with a _when_ clause. Change the verbs to the correct tense.**

1. (my stepson / travel / to Spain / when / he / finish / college)

   _When he finishes college, my stepson will travel to Spain._

2. (I / look / for a full-time job / when / I / graduate / from college)

   _____

3. (he / cook / dinner for the family / when / he / get / home from work)

   _____

4. (Kate / take / her vitamins / when / she / wake up / in the morning)

   _____

**H. Rewrite the sentences using the correct verb tenses and putting *when* in the correct place.**

1. I get a new job                 I move to a new city

_____

2. he studies                       he passes the test

_____

3. she meets with her boss         she asks him for a raise

_____

4. they buy a bigger house         they have more children

_____

5. we register for college          we finish our English class

_____

6. you call me                   we find a time to study together

_____

**I. Write three goals and obstacles below.**

Personal: _____

Obstacle: _____

Educational: _____

Obstacle: _____

Occupational: _____

Obstacle: _____

**J. Combine your goals and obstacles from Exercise I using a time clause with *when*.**

**EXAMPLE:** Goal: *I want to open a bakery.* Obstacle: *I don't have enough money.*
When I *get enough money,* I will *open a bakery.* _____

1. _____

2. _____

3. _____

# LESSON 3 The future

**GOAL** ■ Write about a personal goal

## A. Read the definitions below and write a sentence using each word.

**promotion:** moving up in a job (for example, from store clerk to store manager)

_____

**online class:** a class that you take on the Internet

_____

**quickly:** to do something fast

_____

## B. Look at Patrick's goal chart and read his paragraph.

| Goal | Obstacle | Possible solutions |
|------|----------|--------------------|
| get a promotion at work | need more education | 1. go to school at night<br>2. take online classes |

My goal is to get a promotion at work, but I don't have the education I need to get this promotion. It will be difficult because I work long hours during the day. One solution is to work fewer hours and go to school at night. Another solution is to take online classes that I can do late at night or on the weekend. I really want this promotion, so I need to come up with a solution quickly.

## C. Answer the questions on a separate piece of paper.

1. What is Patrick's goal?

2. What obstacle is in the way of him reaching his goal?

3. What are the solutions to his problem?

4. Which solution do you think is best? Why?

5. Can you come up with another solution?

**D.** The infinitive verb is the base verb with *to* in front of it: *to buy, to eat, to work,* etc. Underline all the infinitive verbs in Patrick's paragraph. How many did you find?

_____

**E.** Study the chart.

| Be + Infinitive | | | | |
|---|---|---|---|---|
| Subject | *Be* | Infinitive | | |
| My goal | is | to get | a job. | The infinitive comes after the verb to express future actions or events such as a hope, a dream, or a goal. |
| One solution | is | to work | part-time. | |
| Another solution | is | to have | my mother help. | |
| My dream | is | to own | my own business. | |

**F.** Circle the correct form of the verb and write the correct infinitive in the space provided.

| | | | |
|---|---|---|---|
| move | ~~get~~ | finish | own |
| ask | become | buy | fix |

1. Matt's dream ((is)/are) _____ to get _____ his college degree in Business Administration.

2. Her hope (is/are) _____ back to Korea after she gets her teaching credential.

3. Their goals (is/are) _____ a new house and bring their family up from Mexico.

4. Eric's dream (is/are) _____ four restaurants in the next five years.

5. His solution (is/are) _____ family and friends for money.

6. Marna and Patrick's hopes (is/are) _____ school and get full-time jobs.

7. My goal (is/are) _____ a United States citizen.

8. His goal (is/are) _____ his grandfather's car.

**G.** **Read Eric's goal chart and complete the sentences.**

| Goal | Obstacle | Possible solutions |
|------|----------|--------------------|
| open a Japanese restaurant | not enough money | 1. get a loan from the bank<br>2. ask friends and family for money<br>3. find private investors |

1. Eric's goal _____.

   His obstacle is he doesn't have enough money.

2. One solution _____.

3. Another solution _____.

4. A third solution _____.

**H.** **Using the information about Eric, write a paragraph about his goal.**

_____

_____

_____

_____

**I.** **Complete the goal chart for yourself. Then, write sentences below.**

| Goal | Obstacle | Possible solutions |
|------|----------|--------------------|
|      |          | 1.<br>2.<br>3. |

1. My goal _____.

   My obstacle is _____.

2. One solution _____.

3. Another solution _____.

4. A third solution _____.

**J.** **On a separate piece of paper, write a paragraph about your goal.**

# LESSON **4** Study habits

**GOAL** ■ Analyze study habits

**A.** A habit is something that you do regularly. What are some habits that you have? Make a list and put each habit in the correct column.

| Good habits | Bad habits |
|---|---|
|  |  |

**B.** Look at the list of study habits.

✓ watching TV while studying
✓ doing your homework on time
✓ rewriting your class notes
✓ copying your friend's homework
✓ studying in a quiet place
✓ asking questions in class
✓ listening to music while studying
✓ studying with a classmate

**C.** Which of the study habits in Exercise B do you think are good? Which do you think are bad? Write each habit in the correct column.

| Good study habits | Bad study habits |
|---|---|
|  |  |

**D.** A gerund is a verb with *–ing* on the end. This verb acts like a noun. Look at the gerunds in your lists in Exercise C.

**E.** Study the chart.

| Be + Gerund | | | | |
|---|---|---|---|---|
| **Subject** | **Be** | **Gerund** | | |
| A good study habit | is | asking | questions in class. | The gerund comes after the verb to express <u>results</u>, <u>solutions</u>, <u>secrets</u>, or <u>keys</u>. |
| A bad study habit | is | copying | your friend's work. | |
| My secret | is | studying | in a quiet place. | |
| My best study habit | is | rewriting | my class notes. | |

**F.** Write the gerund form of each of the verbs below.

1. watch     _watching_____

2. help     _____

3. teach     _____

4. learn     _____

5. study     _____

6. write     _____

7. read     _____

8. listen     _____

9. work     _____

10. find     _____

**G.** Complete each sentence below with a gerund from Exercises E and F.

1. A good study habit is _____ books and magazines in English.

2. A bad study habit is _____ someone else's homework.

3. Jenna's best study habit is _____ what she learns to someone else.

4. Alya's worst study habit is not _____ when her teacher is talking.

5. Aaron's secret to good grades is _____ for two hours every night.

6. Kimber's key to learning English is _____ to the radio in English.

**H.** Look at the study habits. Complete each sentence below with a study habit. Don't forget to change the base verb to a gerund.

| Study Habits | |
|---|---|
| ✓ copy your friend's homework | ✓ ask questions in class |
| ✓ do your homework on time | ✓ listen to music while studying |
| ✓ rewrite your class notes | ✓ study in a quiet place |
| ✓ watch TV while studying | ✓ study with a classmate |

1. Two good study habits are _____

   and _____.

2. Two bad study habits are _____

   and _____.

3. A good classroom study habit is _____.

4. A study habit that a teacher would like is _____

   _____.

5. A study habit that a teacher would *not* like is _____

   _____.

**I.** Now think about your own study habits. Complete each sentence below about yourself. Don't forget to use the verb *Be* and a gerund.

1. My best study habit _____.

2. My worst study habit _____.

3. The study habit I'd like to try _____

   _____.

4. I think the key to learning English _____

   _____.

**GOAL** ■ Manage time

**A.** Write a sentence using each of the words below.

1. organized      _____

2. schedule      _____

3. time      _____

4. accomplish      _____

5. task      _____

6. value      _____

**B.** Read the list of time management strategies.

☐ keep a schedule
☐ write down your tasks
☐ check off each completed task
☐ wake up early
☐ do two things at once
☐ ask friends and family for help
☐ _____
☐ _____

**C.** Which time management strategies do you do? Put a check (✓) in the box in front of each one you follow.

**D.** Add two more strategies to the list.

**E.** Underline each verb in the list of time management strategies. How are they the same?

**F. Study the chart.**

| Imperatives | | | |
|---|---|---|---|
| **Negative** | **Base verb** | | |
|  | Keep | a schedule. | Use the imperative to give instructions or commands. |
|  | Wake up | early. |  |
| Do not | waste | time. | The subject of the imperative is *you* but don't include it in the statement. |
| Don't | forget | your schedule. |  |

**G. Complete each time management strategy with a verb from the box.**

| keep | waste | carry | ~~wake up~~ | write | put | check | ask | finish | do |
|---|---|---|---|---|---|---|---|---|---|

1. _____ Wake up _____ early.

2. _____ friends and family for help.

3. _____ organized.

4. _____ your schedule with you at all times.

5. _____ off each completed task.

6. _____ two things at once.

7. Don't _____ time.

8. _____ everything on your list.

9. _____ a schedule.

10. _____ each task in a time slot.

**H. Write four more time management strategies using imperatives.**

1. _____

2. _____

3. _____

4. _____

**I.  Read about each person's problem with time and suggest two strategies to help.**

1. Eva has a lot of doctor's appointments for herself and her three children, but she can never remember when they are and she often misses them.

    1. _____
    2. _____

2. Franco is so busy with work and school that he can never find time to visit his family and friends.

    1. _____
    2. _____

3. Akiko has a lot of things to do every day. She can never remember everything she has to do and always forgets something.

    1. _____
    2. _____

4. Lubna is so busy taking care of her children that she doesn't have time for herself.

    1. _____
    2. _____

**J.  How do you spend your time? Fill in the percentages.**

Work: _____%

School: _____%

Family: _____%

Exercise: _____%

Entertainment: _____%

TOTAL _____%

**K.  Create a pie chart on a separate piece of paper showing how you spend your time. Make sure your chart equals 100%.**

# PRACTICE TEST

---

## A. Read Bradley's schedule and circle the best answers.

|  | Mon | Tues | Wed | Thurs | Fri | Sat | Sun |
|---|---|---|---|---|---|---|---|
| 6 a.m. | yoga | yoga |  |  | yoga |  |  |
| 8 a.m. | work | work | work | work | work | work |  |
| 10 a.m. | work | work | work | work | work | work |  |
| 12 p.m. | work | work | work | work | work | work |  |
| 2 p.m. | work | work | work | work | work |  |  |
| 4 p.m. | work | work | work | work | work |  |  |
| 6 p.m. | work | work | work | work | work |  |  |
| 8 p.m. | online class |  | online class |  | play volleyball |  |  |

1. What does Bradley do for exercise?

   a. He runs.                    b. He does yoga.

   c. He plays volleyball.        d. He does yoga and plays volleyball.

2. How many days a week does Bradley work?

   a. four                        b. five

   c. six                         d. seven

3. How often is his online class?

   a. twice a week                b. at night

   c. early in the morning        d. once a week

4. What is the best day for Bradley to see his friends and family?

   a. Friday                      b. Sunday

   c. Monday                      d. Thursday

5. How often does Bradley exercise?

   a. three times a week          b. four times a week

   c. twice a week                d. never

# LESSON **1** Shopping for goods and services

**GOAL** ■ Identify places to purchase goods and services

## A. Complete the following two definitions.

1. Goods are _____.

2. Services are _____.

## B. Complete the following lists with ideas of your own.

| Places to purchase goods | Places to purchase services |
|---|---|
| grocery store | hair salon |
| | |
| | |
| | |
| | |

## C. Read the conversation.

**Emily:** Marta, since I'm new here, I'm wondering if you can tell me where you get things done.

**Marta:** Sure, what do you need?

**Emily:** I need to get my work clothes cleaned and some house keys made.

**Marta:** Well, I get my clothes cleaned at Crown Cleaners and my keys made at the hardware store on First Street.

**Emily:** Great! What about a nearby post office and a good place to get a hair cut?

**Marta:** I usually go to the post office on Harbor, and I get my hair cut at Kathy's Salon.

**Emily:** Thanks, Marta. You've been a big help!

**D. Answer the questions about the conversation.**

1. Where does Marta get her clothes cleaned? _____

2. What does Marta do at Kathy's Salon? _____

3. Where can Emily get keys made? _____

4. Where can Emily get her packages mailed? _____

**E. Study the chart.**

| Causative with *get* | | | | | |
|---|---|---|---|---|---|
| Subject | *Get* | Object | Past participle | | Explanation |
| I | get | my car | washed | every Sunday. | *Causative* means that the subject causes something to happen.<br>Any tense of the verb *get* can be used. |
| We | got | our picture | taken. | | |
| They | will get | the roof | fixed | next year. | |

**F. Write the past participles for the following verbs.**

1. clean _____    2. cut _____

3. fix _____    4. fill _____

5. paint _____    6. cash _____

7. wash _____    8. change _____

**G. Unscramble the words to make causative sentences.**

1. refrigerator / I / got / fixed / the _I got the refrigerator fixed._____

2. house / he / the / gets / cleaned / once a week _____

3. she / watch / got / fixed / her / yesterday _____

4. get / their / every year / picture / taken / they _____

5. car / we / will get /repaired / the _____

**H. Rewrite each sentence using a causative with *get*.**

1. My uncle will fix my stereo today.

   I will *get my stereo* fixed *today.* _____

2. The dry cleaner cleaned Terron's coat.

   Terron _____

3. The bank corrected the mistake for me.

   I _____

4. They repair my car at the garage.

   I _____

5. The pharmacist filled Leilani's prescription.

   Leilani _____

6. The mailing center will mail our package.

   Our _____

7. The doctor tests her eyes every year.

   She _____

**I. Write sentences about where you get things done.**

1. wash your car

   _____

2. fill your prescriptions

   _____

3. shorten your pants

   _____

4. cash your check

   _____

5. cut your hair

   _____

6. repair your car or bicycle

   _____

# LESSON ② Advertisements

**GOAL** ■ Interpret advertisements

## A. Match the vocabulary.

1. no charge
2. satisfaction
3. discount
4. guarantee

a. promise
b. free
c. happy with a product or service
d. cheaper than usual

## B. Read the ads about the three different refrigerators for sale.

## C. Answer the questions about the ads.

1. Which refrigerator is the cheapest? _____

2. Which refrigerator is the most expensive? _____

3. Which refrigerator is the largest? _____

4. Which refrigerator is the smallest? _____

5. Which refrigerator would you buy? _____

6. Why would you buy this refrigerator? _____

_____

_____

## D. Study the chart.

| Superlative Adjectives | | | |
|---|---|---|---|
| | **Adjective** | **Superlative** | **Rule** |
| Short | small<br>slow | the smallest<br>the slowest | add –**est** |
| Long | beautiful | the most beautiful | add **the most** before the adjective |
| Adjectives that end in -**e** | large<br>safe | the largest<br>the safest | add -**st** |
| Adjectives that end in –**y** | pretty<br>easy | the prettiest<br>the easiest | change the –**y** to –**i** and add -**est** |
| Adjectives that end in consonant-vowel-consonant | big<br>hot<br>flat | the biggest<br>the hottest<br>the flattest | double the final consonant and add -**est** |
| Irregular | good<br>bad | the best<br>the worst | These adjectives are irregular. |
| *Always use **the** before a superlative. | | | |

## E. Use a superlative adjective to complete each sentence.

1. (good) Office Deals is the _____ *best* _____ place to buy office supplies.

2. (tasty) Which restaurant has the _____ pizza?

3. (beautiful) That clothing boutique has the _____ dresses.

4. (fast) I think the car wash near our house has the _____ service.

5. (popular) Her doctor is the _____ surgeon at Clearview Hospital.

6. (slow) The teller at this bank is the _____ I have ever seen!

7. (easy) These are the _____ directions to the mall.

8. (bad) This refrigerator is the _____ because it doesn't keep food cold.

**F.** Choose an adjective to complete each sentence. Make the adjective superlative. (Note: Adjectives can be used more than once.)

| important | expensive | bad |
| hard | small | hot |

1. Which computer is _____?

2. Remember, the final interview is _____.

3. That restaurant has _____ service.

4. The weather today is _____ we have had all summer.

5. Babyland sells _____ baby clothing I have even seen.

6. This is _____ homework our teacher has ever given us.

**G.** Write superlative questions.

1. (mall / nice / stores) _Which mall has the nicest stores?_____

2. (pharmacy / good) _____

3. (grocery store / big) _____

4. (dry cleaner / good / service) _____

5. (post office / bad / hours) _____

**H.** Think about places in your community. Use the adjectives below to write sentences about places you know.

1. (bad) _____

2. (good) _____

3. (interesting) _____

4. (friendly) _____

5. (cheap) _____

6. (slow) _____

# LESSON ③ Making comparisons

**GOAL** ■ Compare products

**A. Read the ads from the pizza restaurants.**

**B. Answer the questions about the ads.**

1. Which pizza is cheaper? _____

2. Which pizza is more expensive? _____

3. Which pizza is larger? _____

4. Which pizza is smaller? _____

**C. Look at the information about the two stores in Irvine.**

| Shelby's Shoes | The Clothing Depot |
|---|---|
| **Location:** Irvine | **Location:** Irvine |
| **Size:** 1,500 square feet | **Size:** 2,000 square feet |
| **Employees:** 18 | **Employees:** 15 |
| **Proximity to Bus Stop:** 300 feet | **Proximity to Bus Stop:** 100 feet |

**D. Answer the questions.**

1. Which store is closer to the bus stop? _____

2. Which store has more employees? _____

3. Which store is larger? _____

4. Which store is smaller? _____

**E.** **Study the chart.**

| Comparative Adjectives | | | |
|---|---|---|---|
| | Adjective | Comparative | Rule |
| Short | small<br>slow | smaller<br>slower | add –**er** |
| Long | beautiful | more beautiful | add **more** before the adjective |
| Adjectives that end in -**e** | large<br>safe | larger<br>safer | add –**r** |
| Adjectives that end in –**y** | pretty<br>easy | prettier<br>easier | change the –**y** to –**i** and add -**er** |
| Adjectives that end in consonant-vowel-consonant | big<br>hot<br>flat | bigger<br>hotter<br>flatter | double the final consonant and add -**er** |
| Irregular | good<br>bad | better<br>worse | These adjectives are irregular. |

Pontillo's pizza is **bigger than** Angelo's pizza.

Pontillo's has **more employees than** Angelo's pizza.

Note: Notice the placement of *than* after the comparative and the use of more with nouns.

**F.** **Find the mistake in each sentence and correct it.**

1. Going to the car wash is ~~easyer~~ *easier* than washing your own car.

2. I think pizza is healthy than hamburgers.

3. Pontillo's pizza is always more hot than Angelo's pizza.

4. This computer is more heavy than my old one.

5. First Bank is close than Bank of the South.

**G. Use the adjectives to write comparative sentences about the underlined words.**

1. desktop computer / a laptop (expensive)

   A laptop is more expensive than a desktop computer.

2. a 10-inch screen / a 20-inch screen (good)

   _____

3. the mouse pad / the screen size (important)

   _____

**H. Answer the following questions about your community with a long answer and a short answer.**

1. Which grocery store has lower prices?

   Long: Henry's has lower prices than Organic Foods.

   Short: Henry's.

2. Which gas station is closest to your house?

   Long: _____

   Short: _____

3. Which restaurant has better food?

   Long: _____

   Short: _____

4. Which mall has the best stores?

   Long: _____

   Short: _____

5. Which shoe store has more expensive shoes?

   Long: _____

   Short: _____

# LESSON **4** Cash or charge?

**GOAL** ■ Identify and compare purchasing methods

## A. Read the sentences and answer the questions that follow.

1. I *have to* pay my credit card in full every month.

2. I *must* make sure I have enough money in the bank when I write a check.

3. I *have to* keep my cash in a safe place.

4. I *must* deposit my paycheck right when I get it.

What do *must* and *have to* mean? _____

Which one has the stronger meaning? _____

## B. Look at Jared's *to-do list*.

| TO-DO LIST | | |
| --- | --- | --- |
| Monday<br>Go to the bank<br>Pick up dry cleaning<br>File taxes<br>Put out the trash | Tuesday<br>Go to the eye doctor<br>Volunteer at Eli's school<br>Mail package to mom | Wednesday<br>Finish English essay<br>Meet study group |

## C. Answer the questions about Jared. Use *have to* and *must*.

1. What does Jared have to do on Monday?

_____

_____

2. What does he have to do on Tuesday?

_____

_____

3. What must he do on Wednesday?

_____

_____

**D.** We use *must* and *have to* when something is necessary. *Must* is a little stronger than *have to*. Study the chart.

| Must and Have to | | | | |
|---|---|---|---|---|
| **Subject** | **Modal** | **Base verb** | | |
| Jared | has to | go | to the bank. | *Must* and *have to* show necessity. |
| We | have to | meet | at the restaurant at 5 p.m. | |
| Jared | must | finish | his English essay before class on Tuesday. | |
| They | must | help | their parents move tomorrow. | |

**E.** Unscramble the words to make statements of necessity. Change the verb if necessary.

1. register / must / class / we / for / soon

   We must register for class soon.

2. deposit / she / have / her / to / today / check

   _____

3. must / locks / they / changed / their / on / get / the / house

   _____

4. Jared / file / must / taxes / his / Monday / on

   _____

5. have / buy / to / computer / new / for / a / he / school

   _____

6. must / Elise / dry cleaning / pick/ the / up / work / before

   _____

7. see / we / doctor / to / the / have / week / next

   _____

8. open / have / we / to / bank account / a

   _____

**F.** Complete the sentences of necessity in the paragraph with verbs from the box. Don't forget to include *must* or *have to*.

| buy | get | write | pay | go | apply |
|-----|-----|-------|-----|-----|-------|

Terron and Leilani always (1) _____ cash out of the ATM. Leilani

(2) _____ for groceries and school supplies for the kids, and

Terron (3) _____ lunch and dinners out. Sometimes, Leilani

(4) _____ a personal check if she runs out of cash. Terron thinks

they (5) _____ for a credit card and Leilani agrees. So, Terron

(6) _____ to the bank tomorrow and fill out an application.

**G.** Complete the chart with the things you *have to* do and *must* do this month.

| Have to | Must |
|---------|------|
|         |      |
|         |      |
|         |      |
|         |      |

**H.** What do you *have to* do this month? Write 3 sentences.

1. _____

2. _____

3. _____

**I.** What *must* you do this month? Write 3 sentences.

1. _____

2. _____

3. _____

# LESSON **5** Think before you buy

**GOAL** ■ Make a smart purchase

**A. What does each of the words below mean to you? Write a short definition.**

1. plan: _____

2. save: _____

3. purchase: _____

4. comparison shop: _____

5. think: _____

**B. Put the steps from Exercise A in the correct order to make a smart purchase.**

1. _____

2. _____

3. _____

4. _____

5. _____

**C. Put the following steps for buying a car in the correct order (1–5).**

_____ Buy the car.

_____ Decide which kind of car you want.

_____ Negotiate with the car dealer.

_____ Look around for the best price.

_____ Decide to buy a new car.

**D.** When telling or writing a story or describing a process, we use transition words. Study the chart.

| Transition Words | | |
|---|---|---|
| **Numbers** | **Without numbers** | |
| First, (First of all,) | First, | • Do not use numbers as transition words if there are more than four steps. |
| Second, | Next, | • When not using numbers, **Next, Then,** and **After that** can be used in any order and to describe more than one step. |
| Third, | Then, | • Always finish with the words **Finally** or **Lastly**. |
| | After that, | |
| Finally, (Lastly,) | Finally, | |

**E.** Complete the paragraph below with transition words.

_____, you make a decision to buy a new car. _____, you

decide what kind of car you want. _____, you look around for the best price.

_____, you negotiate with the car dealer. _____, you buy the car.

**F.** Use the following sentences to write two different paragraphs. Add transition words that use ordinal numbers (first, second, third, etc.) at the beginning of the sentences.

Make your purchases.
Visit each store.
~~Ask your friends where they get their clothes.~~
Compare prices of similar items.

**Buying New Clothes**

First, ask your friends where they get their clothes. _____

_____

_____

_____

_____

Decide if this is the right bank for you.

Choose a bank near your home.

Talk to the bank manager.

Go home and think about what the manager said.

**Finding the Right Bank**

_____

_____

_____

_____

_____

**G.** **Complete the sentences with transition words. More than one transition word may be correct for some sentences.**

Buying a car could cost you a lot of money. (1) _____, you need to find

a car that you can afford. (2) _____, you'll need to pay for license and

registration. (3) _____, you need to find insurance that is in your budget.

(4) _____, you can start thinking how to pay for gas and all regular maintenance.

(5) _____, you may need to pay for things such as parking and toll roads.

(6) _____, you'll need to start saving money for emergency repairs that may

come up. Owning a car can be very expensive!

**H.** **Using transition words, write a paragraph about a large purchase that you made.**

_____

_____

_____

_____

_____

**A.** Read and choose the best answer.

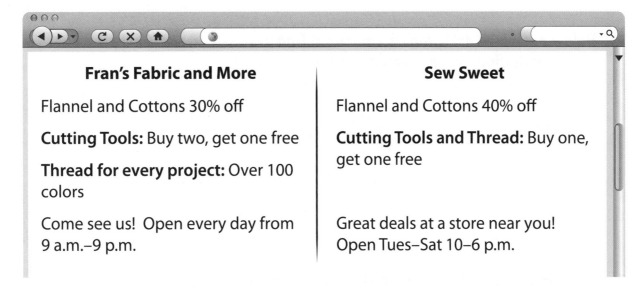

1. What type of store are these ads from?
   a. department store
   b. sewing and fabric store
   c. cutting machines and tools store
   d. sporting goods store

2. Which store is open longer?
   a. Fran's Fabric and More
   b. Sew Sweet
   c. They are both open the same number of hours.
   d. The ads don't say.

3. Which store has a better discount on flannel?
   a. Fran's Fabric and More
   b. Sew Sweet
   c. They are selling flannel for the same price.
   d. Flannel is not on sale.

4. If you need more than one pair of scissors, which store could you shop at?
   a. Fran's Fabric and More
   b. Sew Sweet
   c. It doesn't matter.
   d. These stores don't sell scissors.

# LESSON **1** House hunting

**GOAL** ■ Interpret classified ads

**A.** Below are words and phrases you might find in classified ads. Circle the ones you know. Underline the ones you don't know.

| | | | |
|---|---|---|---|
| appliances | included | available | balcony |
| washer/dryer hookups | community pool | security deposit | |

_____        _____

_____        _____

_____        _____

**B.** Look at the ads below. Add words to the list in Exercise A.

**CONDO FOR RENT**
Three-bedroom, two-bathroom condo with a two-car garage, small yard, and all appliances included. No pets allowed.
$1,700/mo

View          Contact Agent

**SPACIOUS APARTMENT**
Four-bedroom, two-bathroom apartment on the second floor with a community pool.
No appliances but utilities paid.
Pets OK with a $250 deposit.
$2,000/month plus a security deposit

View          Contact Agent

**C.** Answer the questions about the ads.

1. Which place is more expensive, the condo or the apartment?

_____

2. Which place has more bedrooms?

_____

3. Which place has more bathrooms?

_____

4. Which place has the fewest appliances?

_____

**D. Study the chart.**

| Comparatives and Superlatives with Nouns | |
|---|---|
| **Comparatives using nouns** | **Explanation** |
| The apartment has *more bedrooms* than the condo. | Use *more* or *fewer* to compare count nouns. |
| The condo has *fewer bedrooms* than the apartment. | |
| The condo gets *more sun* than the apartment. | Use *more* or *less* to compare non-count nouns. |
| The apartment gets *less light* than the condo. | |
| The condo has *the most bathrooms*. | Use *the most* or the *fewest* for count nouns. |
| The apartment has *the fewest appliances*. | |
| The condo has *the most space* outdoors. | Use *the most* or *the least* for non-count nouns. |
| The apartment has *the least space* outdoors. | |

**E. Use one of the expressions in the box to complete each sentence.**

| more | fewer | less | the most | the fewest | the least |
|---|---|---|---|---|---|

1. The Rivera family pays $1,550 rent and the Browns pay $1,000.

   The Browns pay _____ less _____ rent than the Riveras.

2. The Browns' apartment has three bedrooms and the Riveras' has two.

   The Riveras' apartment has _____ bedrooms.

3. The Riveras have two bathrooms and the Browns have three.

   The Riveras have _____ bathrooms than the Browns.

4. The Riveras' place is very sunny but the Browns' isn't.

   The Browns' place gets _____ light.

5. The Browns' apartment has all appliances but the Riveras' only has a stove.

   The Browns have _____ appliances.

6. The Browns spend more money on rent than the Riveras.

   At the end of the month, the Browns have _____ money than the Riveras.

**F.** **Correct the error in each sentence.**

              *more*
1. We have ~~most~~ problems with our landlord than you do.

2. We have the few apartments in our building than you do.

3. I pay less rent of anyone in my family.

4. His condo has the most space than his friend's.

5. Her house gets the more light.

6. Their apartment has most bathrooms than your apartment.

**G.** **Write two ads: one for the Browns' apartment and one for the Riveras'. Use the information from Exercise E.**

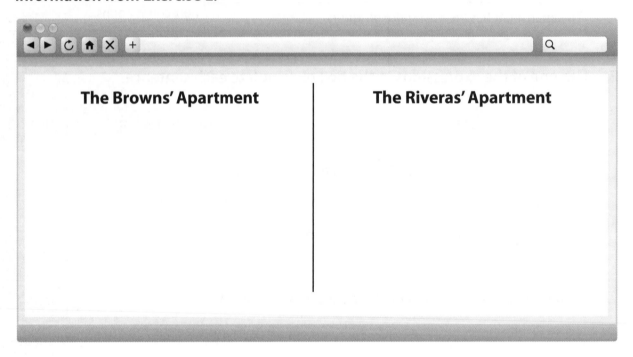

**The Browns' Apartment**          **The Riveras' Apartment**

**H.** **Which apartment would you rather rent?** _____
**Write four sentences using comparatives to explain your choice.**

1. _____

2. _____

3. _____

4. _____

# LESSON **2** Time to move

**GOAL** ■ Make decisions

## A. Write definitions for the words.

1. balcony _____

2. tennis court _____

3. garage _____

4. hardwood floors _____

5. washer/dryer _____

6. security guard _____

7. carport _____

8. refrigerator _____

## B. Look at the Clarkes' housing preferences.

| | | | |
|---|---|---|---|
| ☐ 2 bedrooms | ☑ garage | ☑ air conditioning | ☐ Jacuzzi |
| ☑ 3 bedrooms | ☐ carport | ☑ heating | ☐ balcony |
| ☐ 4 bedrooms | ☑ yard | ☐ refrigerator | ☑ hardwood floors |
| ☑ 2 bathrooms | ☐ pool | ☑ washer/dryer | ☐ high ceilings |
| ☐ 3 bathrooms | ☐ tennis courts | ☐ carpet | ☐ security guard |

## C. Answer the questions about the Clarkes' housing preferences.

1. Do the Clarkes want a yard? _____

2. Do they want four bedrooms? _____

3. Do they want hardwood floors? _____

4. Do they want a refrigerator? _____

## D. Study the chart.

| Present Tense *Yes/No* Questions and Answers | | | | |
|---|---|---|---|---|
| *Do/Does* | Subject | Base verb | | Answer |
| Do | I<br>you<br>we<br>they | have | a pool?<br>four bedrooms?<br>air conditioning?<br>a garage? | Yes, I do.<br>No, you don't.<br>Yes, we do.<br>No, they don't. |
| Does | he<br>she | want | a bigger place?<br>a yard for her dog? | Yes, he does.<br>No, she doesn't. |

## E. Complete each question and answer with the correct word: *do, does, don't, doesn't.*

1. _____ Does _____ he need three bathrooms? Yes, he _____ does _____.

2. _____ you want more bedrooms? Yes, we _____.

3. _____ he have a balcony? No, he _____.

4. _____ their family live in a house? Yes, they _____.

5. _____ we need a yard? Yes, we _____.

6. _____ she have a two-story place. No, she _____.

## F. Use the words to write *yes/no* questions. Then, answer the questions.

1. The Browns / want a bigger apartment

   <u>Do the Browns want a bigger apartment?</u> _____ Yes, <u>they do</u> _____.

2. Eric / have a place with a pool

   _____ No, _____.

3. their family / need a garage

   _____ Yes, _____.

4. they / hope to find a condo

   _____ Yes, _____.

5. Karla / want hardwood floors

   _____ No, _____.

6. he / have a place with a pool

   _____ Yes, _____.

**G.** Write *yes/no* questions to ask someone about his or her housing preferences. Use the checklist in Exercise H if you need ideas.

1. Do you want two bedrooms? _____

2. _____

3. _____

4. _____

5. _____

6. _____

7. _____

8. _____

**H.** Imagine you have a friend who has a family with three kids and two dogs. Complete the checklist below for what his or her family would need.

☐ 2 bedrooms     ☐ garage     ☐ air conditioning     ☐ Jacuzzi
☐ 3 bedrooms     ☐ carport     ☐ heating     ☐ balcony
☐ 4 bedrooms     ☐ yard     ☐ refrigerator     ☐ hardwood floors
☐ 2 bathrooms     ☐ pool     ☐ washer/dryer     ☐ high ceilings
☐ 3 bathrooms     ☐ tennis courts     ☐ carpet     ☐ security guard

**I.** Based on your housing preferences and those of your friend's from Exercise H, complete the Venn Diagram.

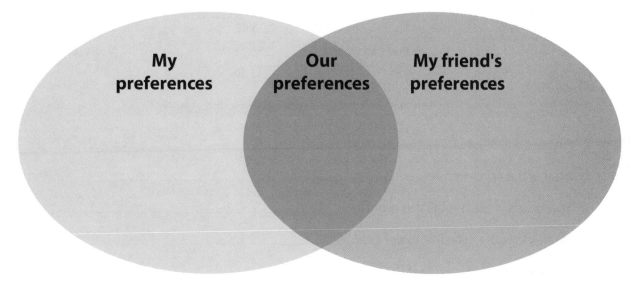

# LESSON ③ Paying the bills

GOAL ■ Arrange and cancel utilities

## A. Match each question word with the type of answer.

1. Who/Whose?          a. a time or date
2. What?               b. an amount (time, money, etc.)
3. Where?              c. a person
4. When?               d. a reason
5. Why?                e. a location
6. How much?           f. a thing

## B. Read the gas bill and answer the questions below.

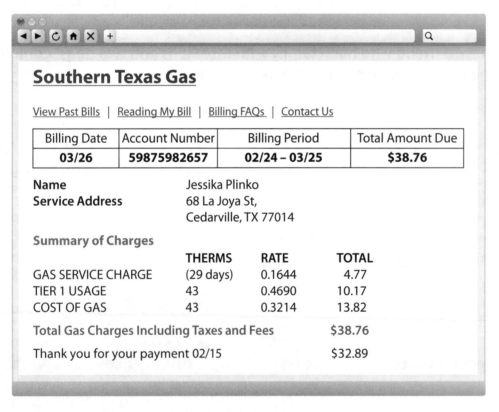

### Southern Texas Gas

View Past Bills | Reading My Bill | Billing FAQs | Contact Us

| Billing Date | Account Number | Billing Period | Total Amount Due |
|---|---|---|---|
| 03/26 | 59875982657 | 02/24 – 03/25 | $38.76 |

**Name**         Jessika Plinko
**Service Address**   68 La Joya St,
                Cedarville, TX 77014

**Summary of Charges**

|  | THERMS | RATE | TOTAL |
|---|---|---|---|
| GAS SERVICE CHARGE | (29 days) | 0.1644 | 4.77 |
| TIER 1 USAGE | 43 | 0.4690 | 10.17 |
| COST OF GAS | 43 | 0.3214 | 13.82 |
| Total Gas Charges Including Taxes and Fees | | | $38.76 |
| Thank you for your payment 02/15 | | | $32.89 |

1. Whose bill is this? _____

2. What is the account number? _____

3. How much is the gas bill this month? _____

4. Where does the account holder live? _____

5. When was the last payment? _____

**C.** Underline the question words in Exercise B.

**D.** Study the chart.

| Information Question Words | | |
|---|---|---|
| **Question word** | **Answer** | **Example** |
| Who | person | Jessika |
| What | thing (account number) | 59875982657 |
| Where | place | Texas |
| When | time or date | February 20th or 10 a.m. |
| How much | amount of something (money, time, etc.) | $32.89 |

**E.** Match each question word to two correct answers.

_____ 1.  Who                    a. $125.68

_____                            b. Vietnam

_____ 2.  What                  c. 4:30 p.m.

_____                            d. Brian Davis

_____ 3.  Where               e. gas bill

_____                            f. 20 minutes

_____ 4.  When                g. 598798561324

_____                            h. Rogelio

_____ 5.  How much         i. November 1, 2003

_____                            j. New York City

**F.** Write the correct question word(s) at the beginning of each question.

1. **Q:** _How much_____ is your water bill?      **A:** $14.67

2. **Q:** _____ is your bill due?      **A:** next week

3. **Q:** _____ do you send your bill?      **A:** 2456 Lyn Road

4. **Q:** _____ was your bill last month?      **A:** $37.14

5. **Q:** _____ does this bill belong to?      **A:** my sister

6. **Q:** _____ does your mail come?      **A:** around 1:30 p.m

7. **Q:** _____ is your gas meter?      **A:** in front of the house

**G.** **Write information questions using the bill.**

**INTERNET ONE**

View Past Bills | Reading My Bill | Billing FAQs | Contact Us

| Billing Date | Account Number | Total Amount Due |
|---|---|---|
| **1/27** | **452-000-438-0002-18** | **$94.99** |

**Name** Bradley Smith
**Service Address** 123 La Joya St,
Cedarville, TX 77014

**ACCOUNT SUMMARY**

| | |
|---|---|
| Previous Balance | $94.99 |
| Payment 01/22 | -$94.99 |
| Balance Forward | $.00 |

**New Charges**

| | |
|---|---|
| Current Activity | $94.99 |
| Total new charges due by 02/21 | |
| TOTAL AMOUNT DUE | $94.99 |

1. Where _____?

2. What _____?

3. Whose _____?

4. When _____?

5. How much _____?

**H.** **Write answers to the questions you wrote in Exercise G.**

1. _____

2. _____

3. _____

4. _____

5. _____

# LESSON **4** How much can we spend?

**GOAL** ■ Create a budget

## A. Answer the questions about budgeting.

1. What is the difference between *income* and *expenses*?

_____

_____

2. What is a *budget*?

_____

3. What are *finances*?

_____

## B. Read about Maryanne and Vu.

Last night, Maryanne and Vu were talking about their finances. Vu was writing down everything they spent money on last month. Maryanne was trying to help him. They were both worrying about how much money they spent on their phone bill. Fortunately, they had extra money from somewhere else. They realized how important it is to budget every month.

## C. Answer the questions.

1. What were Maryanne and Vu doing last night?

_____

2. What was Vu doing?

_____

3. What was Maryanne doing?

_____

4. What were they both doing?

_____

## D. Underline the verbs in the first four sentences. How are they the same?

_____

**E.** **Study the chart.**

| Past Continuous | | | | |
|---|---|---|---|---|
| **Subject** | ***Be*** **(past)** | **Verb +** ***ing*** | | |
| I | was | working | on my budget. | The past continuous describes what was in progress at a specific moment in the past. |
| Vu | was | writing | everything down. | |
| Maryanne | was | trying | to help. | |
| They | were | worrying | about their phone bill. | |

**F.** **Unscramble the words to make past continuous statements. Change the verb** ***Be*** **to the correct form.**

1. writing / they / their / be / budget / down

   They were writing down their budget.

2. saving / I / be / new / for / money / car / a

3. he / jobs / be / working / two

4. adding / numbers / be / up / Vu / the

5. making / be / more / year / money / they / last

6. their / copy / Maryanne / a / making / be / budget / of

**G.** **Complete the sentences with the past continuous form of the verbs.**

| write | add | sit | pay | think | talk |
|---|---|---|---|---|---|

Last night, Maryanne and Vu _____ in the living room. They _____ some bills. They _____ also _____ about their finances. Maryanne _____ down all of their expenses. Vu _____ up the numbers. They _____ about what they would like to save money for: college for the kids, a new home, and a vacation.

**H.** Look at the Hershfields' budget. How much are their total expenses?

| EXPENSES | |
|---|---|
| Rent | $2,500 |
| **Utilities** | |
| Gas | $125 |
| Telephone | $250 |
| Cable TV | $200 |
| Internet | $75 |
| **Food** | |
| Groceries | $600 |
| Dining out | $800 |
| **Entertainment** | $900 |
| **Auto** | |
| Gas and maintenance | $150 |
| Car loan | $450 |
| Insurance | $225 |
| Registration | $285 |
| **Total Expenses** | $ |

**I.** The Hershfields need to cut down their budget. In your opinion, what are three things they could spend less money on?

1. _____

2. _____

3. _____

**J.** Write sentences about the Hershfields' budget that were true before they made budget cuts.

1. (spend) The Hershfields were spending too much money on entertainment._____

2. (dine) _____

3. (watch) _____

4. (pay) _____

5. _____

6. _____

# LESSON **5** Tenant rights

**GOAL** ■ Write a formal letter

## A. Complete each sentence with the best word.

| repair | do-it-yourself (DIY) | complain |
|---|---|---|
| electrician | plumber | renter's insurance |

1. She complained to her landlord about the clogged shower. He called a _____ to fix it.

2. Who can we call to _____ our refrigerator?

3. After calling repair people too many times, we decided to get _____.

4. When I needed to replace a broken light fixture, I called an _____.

5. My brother is a(n) _____ guy who likes to do household repairs and improvements.

## B. Read the sentences and decide which are short actions and which are long actions. Write *short* or *long* beneath each clause.

1. I saw a mouse while I was cleaning.

   _____short_____      _____long_____

2. While I was brushing my teeth, the water shut off.

   _____      _____

3. I saw a crack in the wall while I was hanging a painting.

   _____      _____

4. While they were sleeping, the phone rang.

   _____      _____

5. While he was taking a shower, the water got cold.

   _____      _____

6. The shelf fell down while we were painting the cabinet.

   _____      _____

## C. Circle the correct answers about the sentences in Exercise B.

1. Look at all the short actions. Which verb tense is used?

   a. past      b. past continuous

2. Look at all the long actions. Which verb tense is used?

   a. past      b. past continuous

## D. Study the chart.

| Past Continuous with *while* | | | |
|---|---|---|---|
| **Short action** | ***While*** | **Long action** | **Shorter action** |
| The phone rang | while | she was studying. | |
| I saw a mouse | | I was cleaning. | |
| The oven broke | | they were cooking. | |
| | While | she was studying, | the phone rang. |
| | | I was cleaning, | I saw a mouse. |
| | | they were cooking, | the oven broke. |

- Use the *past continuous* to talk about things that started in the past and continued for a period of time.
- Use the *simple past* to talk about a short action that happened once.
- To connect two events that happened in the past, use the past continuous with *while* for the longer event. Use the simple past for the shorter event.

**Note:** You can reverse the two clauses, but you need a comma if *while* comes first.

## E. Put *while* in the correct place in each of the sentences below.

1. ___While___ he was sleeping, _____ the phone rang.

2. _____ we bought a condo _____ we were living in a rental apartment.

3. _____ my husband was painting the condo, _____ I took our children to the park.

4. _____ I was taking a shower, _____ the water heater broke.

5. _____ the kids found a rat _____ they were playing upstairs.

6. _____ we cooked dinner _____ the repair person was fixing the water heater.

7. _____ we were sleeping, _____ the fire alarm went off.

8. _____ the children and I were waiting outside, my husband looked for smoke.

## F. Combine the sentences.

1. Our heater was being fixed. We wore warm clothes and used extra blankets at night.

   While _our heater was being fixed, we wore warm clothes and used extra blankets at night_.

2. Kimla was calculating last month's expenses. Her children called for help.

   While _____

3. His roof started leaking. He was reading the newspaper.

   While _____.

## G. Combine the sentences using *while*.

1. It started to rain. We were standing on the balcony.

   While _we were standing on the balcony, it started to rain._ _____

2. I was talking with the security guard in our building. She got a phone call.

   _____

3. The rain stopped. We were looking out the window.

   _____

4. I was doing the laundry. The dryer broke.

   _____

5. I saw you. You were leaving the house.

   _____

6. I was cleaning the living room. I turned on the air conditioning.

   _____

## H. Complete each sentence with your own ideas.

1. The lights went out while _I was reading_ _____.

2. While we were eating dinner, _____.

3. _____ while I was studying.

4. While I was driving to school today, _____.

5. The rain stopped while _____.

# PRACTICE TEST

## A. Read and choose the best answer.

### Jacksons' Expenses

| | |
|---|---|
| Rent | $1800 |
| **Utilities** | |
| Gas | $65 |
| Telephone | $125 |
| Cable TV | $100 |
| Internet | $75 |
| **Food** | |
| Groceries | $440 |
| Dining out | $200 |
| **Auto** | |
| Gas and maintenance | $150 |
| Car loan | $300 |
| Insurance | $225 |
| Registration | $132 |
| **Total Expenses** | $ |

1. What is the Jacksons' biggest expense?

   a. rent
   b. utilities
   c. food
   d. auto

2. What is their cheapest utility?

   a. gas
   b. telephone
   c. cable TV
   d. Internet

3. Which statement is true?

   a. They spend more on groceries than dining out.

   b. They spend more on food than auto.

   c. They spend more on cable TV than telephone.

   d. They spend more on insurance than their car loan.

4. What are their total monthly expenses?

   a. $1,800
   b. $3,600
   c. $3,310
   d. $3,612

# LESSON ❶ Places in your community

GOAL ■ Ask for information

**A.** **Read the list of places. Circle the places you regularly go to.**

| | | | |
|---|---|---|---|
| bank | post office | dry cleaners | _____ |
| auto repair shop | gas station | print shop | _____ |
| bookstore | medical office | coffee shop | _____ |
| grocery store | home improvement store | | |

**B.** **Add three more places to the list.**

**C.** **Make a to-do list of things you need to do this week.**

| To-Do List |
|---|
| ☐  *Grocery shopping* |
| ☐ |
| ☐ |
| ☐ |
| ☐ |
| ☐ |

**D.** **Think about the following questions.**

1. Where will you go to do each task on your list?
2. When do you think each place opens?
3. How much will it cost to do each task?

**E.** **Use your list in Exercise C to complete the table.**

| To-do | Where? | When? | How much? |
|---|---|---|---|
| | | | |
| | | | |
| | | | |
| | | | |
| | | | |

**F.** **Study the chart on how to ask information questions.**

| Information Questions | | | |
|---|---|---|---|
| **Question words** | **Verb** | **Singular noun** | **Plural noun** |
| Location | | | |
| Where<br>How far | is | the bank?<br>the school from here? | |
| What | is | the address? | |
| Where<br>How far | are | | the stores?<br>the schools from here? |
| What | are | | the addresses? |
| Time | | | |
| When<br>What time<br>How often | does | the library open?<br>the restaurant close?<br>the bus come? | |
| When<br>What time<br>How often | do | | the stores open?<br>the restaurants close?<br>the buses come? |
| Cost | | | |
| How much | does | it cost? | |
| | do | | the tickets cost? |

**G.** **Complete each sentence with the correct form of *be* or *do*.**

1. What _____*are*_____ the addresses of the two libraries?

2. Where _____ the DMV?

3. What time _____ the restaurants close?

4. What _____ the address of the bookstore?

5. How much _____ the textbooks for this class cost?

6. Where _____ the closest markets?

7. How often _____ the clothing store have a sale?

8. When _____ the hair salon open on Saturdays?

**H.  Write a question for each answer below.**

1. **Q:** What time does the pizza place close? _____

   **A:** The pizza place closes at 10:00 p.m.

2. **Q:** _____

   **A:** The copy center opens at 8:00 a.m.

3. **Q:** _____

   **A:** The address of the museum is 567 Atlantic Boulevard.

4. **Q:** _____

   **A:** The school is four miles from here.

5. **Q:** _____

   **A:** A new driver's license costs $24.

6. **Q:** _____

   **A:** The bus comes every 20 minutes.

**I.  Look back at your to-do list in Exercise C. Choose two places and write three questions you could ask about that place.**

**Place:** The post office

1. Where is the post office?
2. What time does the post office open?
3. How much does it cost to send a package?

**Place:** _____

1. _____

2. _____

3. _____

**Place:** _____

1. _____

2. _____

3. _____

# LESSON **②** The bank, the library, and the DMV

**GOAL** ■ Interpret charts and compare information

## A. Match the word or phrase to the correct meaning.

1. service fee            automatic teller machine

2. ATM                money your account earns for being in the bank

3. online banking       using your telephone to do bank transactions

4. telephone banking    money you pay for having a bank account

5. interest             using the Internet to do bank transactions

## B. Look at the Bank of Vista brochure.

## BANK OF VISTA ▲▲

| | Bank of Vista Regular Checking | Bank of Vista Total Checking | Bank of Vista Plus Checking |
|---|---|---|---|
| Access to 18,000 ATMs and 5,500 branches | yes | yes | yes |
| Online banking | no | yes | yes |
| Telephone banking | no | yes | yes |
| Debit card | yes | yes | yes |
| Fees at non-Bank of Vista ATMs | $2.50 per transaction | no fee 4 times per month, $2.50 per transaction after that | unlimited transactions with no fees |
| Earns interest | no | yes | yes |
| Monthly service fee | $0 | $10 | $25 |

## C. Answer the questions about the information in the brochure.

1. What is the monthly service fee for the Total Checking account? _____

2. What is the ATM fee for the Regular Checking account? _____

3. How much are the ATM fees for the Plus Checking account? _____

4. How much does having a Total Checking account cost each month? _____

## D. Which account would you choose? Why?

_____

_____

## E. Study the chart.

| Information Questions about Cost | | | | | |
|---|---|---|---|---|---|
| Question words | Verb | Singular noun | Plural noun | Base verb | |
| What | is | the fee | | | for the basic account? |
| What | are | | the service fees | | for the accounts? |
| How much | is | the license? | | | |
| How much | are | | the books? | | |
| How much | does | it | | cost? | |
| How much | do | | the tickets | cost? | |

## F. Complete each question with the correct form of *be* or *do*.

1. What _____ are _____ the late fees for library books that are one week late?

2. What _____ the prices for different types of stamps?

3. How much _____ the bank charge for late fees?

4. What _____ the cost of a replacement ATM card?

5. How much _____ the textbooks for this class cost?

6. How much _____ the registration?

**G.** Unscramble the words to make questions. Change the *be* or *do* verb to the correct form.

1. be / what / late payments / for / the charges

   *What are the charges for late payments?*

2. be / what / for / new students / the / fees

   _____

3. much / school lunch / how / do / cost

   _____

4. library card / what / a / be / of / price / the

   _____

5. boxes / do / how / cost / much / mailing / the

   _____

**H.** Look at the information about the post office and match. More than one answer may be correct. Match all that apply.

| Quick Mail Express | Quick Mail | First Class | Standard Mail | Commercial Mail |
|---|---|---|---|---|
| from $16.95 | from $5.75 | from .49 | from $5.60 | from $2.69 |
| 1–2 days or overnight | 1–3 days | estimated 1–3 days | estimated 2–8 days | estimated 2–8 days |

1. First Class            from $5.75
2. Quick Mail            1–3 days
3. Commercial Mail            from $5.60
4. Standard Mail            2–8 days
5. Quick Mail Express            from $16.95

**I.** Use the information above to write questions.

1. *How much does it cost to send a first-class letter?*

2. _____

3. _____

4. _____

# LESSON ③ Finding places

---

**GOAL** ■ Interpret a road map

## A. Look at the expressions used to give directions.

**Turn:** left, right

**Make:** a left, a right

**Go:** left, right, straight, north, south, east, west

**Take:** the exit, the street, the highway

**Get on:** the highway, the street

## B. Look at the map. Follow the directions below.

1. Start at the sushi restaurant on Arizona Street. Go to Second Avenue and turn right. What is the next street?

   _____

2. Start at the shoe store on Colorado Street. Go to Second Avenue and turn left. What is the next street?

   _____

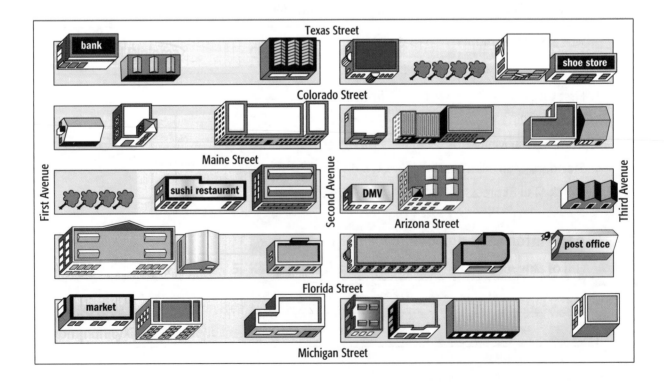

**C.** **Follow the directions using the map in Exercise B. Write the name of the place.**

1. Start at the corner of Third Avenue and Michigan Street. Go straight on Michigan Street. Turn right on Second Avenue. Turn left on Maine Street. Turn right on First Avenue. Go past Colorado Street. What is on the right side? _____

2. Start at the corner of First Avenue and Texas Street. Go straight on Texas Street. Turn right on Second Avenue. Turn left on Arizona Street. Go to the end of the street. What is on the right side? _____

3. Start at the corner of First Avenue and Michigan Street. Go straight on Michigan Street. Turn left on Second Avenue. What is at the corner of Second Avenue and Arizona Street? _____

**D.** **Study the chart below.**

| Imperatives | | | |
|---|---|---|---|
| **Negative** | **Base verb** | | **Explanation** |
| | Go | left. | • Use the imperative to give directions. |
| Don't | turn | right. | • The subject of the imperative is **you** but don't include it in the statement. |
| | Take | the next exit. | • For negative imperatives, **do not** is stronger |
| Do not | get | on the highway. | than **don't**. |

**E.** **Complete each sentence with an imperative. There may be more than one correct answer.**

| turn | make | go | take |
|---|---|---|---|

1. _____ left on State Street.

2. _____ the highway heading south.

3. Don't _____ a right on Biscayne Boulevard.

4. _____ Jay Avenue to the first stop light.

5. _____ right when you see the post office.

6. Do not _____ south on the freeway.

**F. Sometimes, more than one imperative can complete a sentence. Using the imperatives from Exercise E, write all of the possible answers.**

1. _____ left.

2. _____ north.

3. _____ a right.

4. _____ the street.

**G. Use the map in Exercise B to write directions to the following locations.**

1. **From:** the market          **To:** the post office

   From the market, turn right onto Florida Street. Turn left on Third Avenue. Go one block. The

   post office is on the left-hand side on the corner of Third Avenue and Arizona Street.

2. **From:** the sushi restaurant     **To:** the shoe store

   _____

   _____

3. **From:** the DMV          **To:** the market

   _____

   _____

4. **From:** the bank          **To:** the post office

   _____

   _____

**H. Write directions to your home from your school.**

_____

_____

_____

_____

# LESSON 4 Getting things done!

**GOAL** ■ Identify daily activities

## A. Match the expression to an item that completes the phrase. More than one answer is acceptable.

1. drop off                                          the books

2. pick up                                           the post office

3. get _____ ready      the dry cleaning

4. stop by                                          the kids

5. get _____ dressed    some groceries

                                                     the bank

## B. Read about Chinh's day.

> Yesterday was a busy day for Chinh. After she woke up, she took a shower and had breakfast. Before her kids left for school, she packed their lunches and made them breakfast. Then Chinh left for work. After work, she went to the bank to get some cash and then to the dry cleaners to pick up uniforms. Before she picked up the kids from school, she stopped by the bookstore to get a book for her class. Then she dropped the kids off at home with her husband and left for school. She was tired when she got home that night!

## C. What did Chinh do yesterday? Make a list in the correct order.

1. _____      2. _____

3. _____      4. _____

5. _____      6. _____

7. _____      8. _____

9. _____      10. _____

11. _____     12. _____

## D. Study the chart.

| Adverbial Clauses with *Before*, *After*, and *When* | |
|---|---|
| **Rule** | **Example sentences** |
| A comma separates an adverbial clause that comes before the main clause. | **After she woke up,** she took a shower.<br><br>**Before she stopped by the dry cleaners,** she went to the bank.<br><br>**When she got home,** she was tired. |
| A comma is not used when the adverbial clause comes after the main clause. | She took a shower **after she woke up.**<br><br>She went to the bank **before she stopped by the dry cleaners.**<br><br>She was tired **when she got home.** |

## E. Match each main clause with the best time clause.

1. I made an appointment for the road test ___e___.

2. I left home early and the DMV opened just _____.

3. There were not a lot of people in line _____.

4. I was really nervous _____.

5. I felt much better _____.

6. I picked up my license _____.

7. I gave all my friends rides to school _____.

8. I walked everywhere _____.

9. I asked my friends to pay for gas _____.

a. before I left the DMV that day

b. after I got my license

c. before I took my test

d. after I arrived

e. after I practiced for several weeks.

f. when I didn't have any money

g. when I got there

h. before I bought my own car

i. after I finished the test.

**F.** **Write sentences with adverbial clauses following the example below. Then, rewrite the sentence, reversing the clauses.**

1. (1) Jacob saved enough money. (2) He bought a new car. (when)

   a. _When Jacob saved enough money, he bought a new car._

   b. _Jacob bought a new car when he saved enough money._

2. (1) Parker opened his own business. (2) He lost his job. (after)

   a. _____

   b. _____

3. (1) Jeeva finished his test. (2) He asked the teacher a question. (before)

   a. _____

   b. _____

4. (1) It stopped raining. (2) The kids went out to play. (when)

   a. _____

   b. _____

**G.** **What did you do yesterday? Make a list.**

1. _____  2. _____

3. _____  4. _____

5. _____  6. _____

7. _____  8. _____

**H.** **Using your list from Exercise G, write a short paragraph on a separate piece of paper about what you did yesterday using time clauses.**

# LESSON  **5** **My town**

**GOAL** ■ Describe a place

**A.** **Correct each sentence and write the problem using the words from the word bank. Words can be used more than once.**

| capital letter | grammar | punctuation | noun form | verb form |
|---|---|---|---|---|

1. bob lives in massachusetts. _____

2. He works at the post office _____

3. bob is married to mary. _____

4. They have two childrens. _____

4. Mary are a teacher. _____

5. Bob and Mary has two cars. _____

**B.** **There are eight mistakes in Gloria's paragraph. Circle each mistake you find.**

There are many reasons why I love my new town, victoria. First, thanks to the great job market in Victoria, my husband got an excellent positions with a computer company. Second, our family can buys a nice house because the houses is very affordable here. third, the neighborhoods is very safe, so I can let my children play in the park with other childrens. Finally, the excellent schools in this area is nationally recognized. I love Victoria so much that I can't ever imagine moving

**C.** **Study the chart.**

| Editing | | |
|---|---|---|
| **Mechanic** | **Rule** | **Examples** |
| Capital letters | Every proper noun should begin with a capital letter. | Gloria lives in Victoria. |
| Nouns | Every noun should be in the correct singular or plural form. | He has a good job. (not *jobs*) They have five children. (not *childrens*) |
| Verbs | Every verb should be in the correct tense and agree with the noun. | Our family can buy a nice house. There are three parks. |
| Punctuation | Every sentence should end with a period, question mark, or exclamation point. | Gloria never wants to move. Where do you live? |

**D.** **There is one mistake in each sentence. Decide if the mistake is a capital letter, noun, verb, or punctuation and write it on the line. Then, correct the mistake.**

        is
1. Florida ~~are~~ a state in the southern part of the United States. ___verb___

2. Our family moved to Florida last summer _____

3. We moved for three reason. _____

4. first of all, we love the weather. _____

5. It are always sunny and warm. _____

6. second, we bought a house near the water. _____

7. Third, our son want to go to college here and we want to be near him when he

    is at school. _____

8. Is there a better reason than that to move _____

**E. Read the paragraph and find the mistakes. Then, complete the information in the table.**

> The Worshams is going to move next summer because scott got a new job. There are many good reason to move for this job. First, he are going to make twice as much money as he made at his previous job. Second, he will have a better job title, supervisor Third, there are more opportunity for his wife to work in this new city. The kids is not very exited because they like their school and friends. but in time, they will get used to it

| Mechanic | Mistake | Correction |
|---|---|---|
| 1. *verb form* | *is* | *are* |
| 2. | | |
| 3. | | |
| 4. | | |
| 5. | | |
| 6. | | |
| 7. | | |
| 8. | | |

**F. Write a paragraph about a place where you would like to move. Explain your reasons why.**

_____

_____

_____

_____

**G. Read your paragraph and circle any mistakes you find. Use the checklist below.**

1. Does every sentence start with a capital letter?
2. Does every sentence end with punctuation?
3. Is every noun in the correct form?
4. Does every verb tense agree with the noun?
5. Are all proper nouns capitalized?

# PRACTICE TEST

---

**A. Read the paragraph and choose the best answers.**

> It is easy to get from the school to the post office. Once you leave the parking lot, turn right on Jester Avenue. Stay on Jester Avenue for two miles. Turn right on Kipling Lane and go two blocks. The post office is on the right.

1. To where are directions being given?
   a. the post office                     b. the school
   c. Jester Avenue                       d. Kipling Lane

2. Which side of the street is the post office on?
   a. the right                           b. the left
   c. the same side as the school         d. straight ahead

**B. Look at the information about the shipping company and choose the best service.**

| Next Day Express | Next Day | Standard | Saver Express | Saver |
|---|---|---|---|---|
| from $49.95 | from $21.95 | from $15.95 | from $10.95 | from $5.95 |
| arrives before 9:00 a.m. | arrives before 5:00 p.m. | arrives in 1–3 days | arrives in 3–5 days | arrives in 7–10 days |

1. I want my parcel to arrive tomorrow afternoon.
   a. Standard                            b. Next Day
   c. Saver Express                       d. Next Day Express

2. I want the cheapest service.
   a. Next Day Express                    b. Standard
   c. Saver                               d. Saver Express

# LESSON **1** The human body

**GOAL** ■ Identify parts of the body

## A. Identify the parts of the body.

| nose | knee | back | hip | ankle | shoulder | chest | foot | stomach | neck |
|------|------|------|-----|-------|----------|-------|------|---------|------|

1. _____  2. _____

3. _____  4. _____

5. _____  6. _____

7. _____  8. _____

9. _____  10. _____

## B. We use adjectives to describe our body. Use the following adjectives to describe the body parts below. More than one answer can be correct.

| sore | broken | sprained | tight |
|------|--------|----------|-------|

1. I have a _____ neck.  2. She has a _____ ankle.

3. He has a _____ back.  4. You have a _____ nose.

5. Jessica has a _____ hip.  6. Mario has a _____ knee.

## C. Study the chart.

| Should | | | | |
|---|---|---|---|---|
| **Subject** | **Modal** | **Base verb** | | |
| I | | go | to the doctor. | |
| You | should | see | the cardiologist. | Use *should* to give advice. |
| Ken | | try | to eat healthier. | |
| They | | lose | some weight. | |

## D. Complete each sentence with *should* and the base form of the infinitive in parentheses.

1. Erin _____*should lose*_____ weight before getting knee surgery. (to lose)

2. The girls _____ on sunscreen when they go to the beach. (to put)

3. You _____ the dermatologist about that rash on your arm. (to call)

4. I _____ prenatal vitamins because I'm trying to get pregnant. (to take)

5. They think their son _____ a psychiatrist to help him understand the divorce. (to visit)

6. Everyone _____ at least eight glasses of water a day. (to drink)

7. Do you think I _____ a new pediatrician for my daughter? (to find)

8. Karen needs new glasses. She _____ an appointment with the optometrist. (to make)

## E. Read the conversation and answer the questions.

**Doctor:** I have your test results back and the tests show that you have diabetes.

**Ken:** I was afraid of that. It's very common in my family. What should I do?

**Doctor:** Well, besides the medication I'm going to give you, you should see a cardiologist to make sure your heart is healthy. I'll have the nurse recommend one for you.

**Ken:** OK. Anything else?

**Doctor:** Yes, you should try to eat healthier, and you should lose some weight.

**Ken:** OK. My wife has been talking about wanting to lose weight so we can start eating healthier together. Thanks, Doc. I'll be sure to see the cardiologist right away.

**Doctor:** Good. I'd like to see you again in two weeks to see how the medication is working. Make sure you schedule an appointment before you leave.

1. What is Ken's health problem?

_____

2. Which part of his body is affected by this?

_____

3. Who does the doctor say Ken should see?

_____

4. What else does the doctor say Ken should do?

_____

## F. Write sentences of advice.

1. My back hurts.     You should stretch. _____

2. Kimiko sprained her ankle. _____

3. She has a toothache. _____

4. Bradley broke his nose. _____

5. I have a sore neck. _____

**GOAL** ■ Communicate symptoms

**A.** Look at the list of symptoms below. Add three more to the list. What would you do if you had those symptoms? Write your ideas.

| Symptoms | What would I do? |
|---|---|
| rash | put on some cream |
| earache | _____ |
| sore throat | _____ |
| _____ | _____ |
| _____ | _____ |
| _____ | _____ |

**B.** Ana is taking her four kids to the pediatrician today. They are all sick. Read the notes she wrote about each of her kids and complete the sentences.

| Child | Problem | How long? |
|---|---|---|
| Kathryn | sore throat | for 3 days |
| Courtney | rash | for 2 weeks |
| Ryland | cold | since last week |
| Tyler | earache | since yesterday |

1. Kathryn has had a _____ for _____.

2. Courtney has had a _____ for _____.

3. Ryland has had a _____ since _____.

4. Tyler has had an _____ since _____.

## C. Study the charts.

| Present Perfect | | | | | |
|---|---|---|---|---|---|
| Subject | *Have* | Past participle | | Period of time | Example sentence |
| I, You, We, They | have | been | sick | since Tuesday | I *have been* sick since Tuesday. |
| She, He, It | has | had | a backache | for two weeks | She *has had* a backache for two weeks. |
| Use the present perfect for events starting in the past and continuing up to the present. | | | | | |

| *Have* | Subject | Past participle | | Period of time | Example question |
|---|---|---|---|---|---|
| Have | I, you, we, they | been | sick | since Tuesday? | *Have* you *been* sick since Tuesday? |
| Has | she, he, it | had | a backache | for two weeks? | *Has* she *had* a backache for two weeks? |

## D. Complete the charts below with the correct past participle form of the verbs.

| Base form | Past tense | Past participle |
|---|---|---|
| visit | visited | |
| take | took | |
| work | worked | |
| walk | walked | |
| go | went | |

| Base form | Past tense | Past participle |
|---|---|---|
| gain | gained | |
| see | saw | |
| eat | ate | *eaten* |
| be | was, were | |
| have | had | |

## E. Choose one of the verbs from Exercise D and complete each sentence below with the correct present perfect form.

1. _____*Has*_____ she _____*eaten*_____ any food today?

2. Dr. Smith _____ at this hospital for ten years.

3. We _____ sick all week.

4. _____ you _____ your sister in the hospital yet?

5. You _____ three pills already today!

6. Peter _____ a cold since last month.

**F.** **Read about Courtney. Underline all the examples of** *for* **and** *since*.

> Courtney has gone to the same doctor since she was 17 years old. She has seen Dr. Makela twice a year since 1995. Dr. Makela has been her doctor for 21 years!
>
> Since last Monday, Courtney has had a very bad cold. She made an appointment with the doctor. She had taken medicine for three days but it wasn't working, and she had not gone to work since Tuesday. Hopefully, Dr. Makela can give her something stronger so she can get better and get back to work.

**G.** **Complete the chart below by writing what comes after** *for* **and** *since* **in the Exercise F paragraphs.**

| for | since |
|---|---|
|  | she was 17 years old |
| Use **_for_** when an action has continued for a certain amount of time. Use **_since_** when an action began at a specific time. | |

**H.** **Complete the sentences using the present perfect of** *be* **and** *for* **and** *since*.

1. I _____ worried about this rash _____ a week.

2. They _____ depressed _____ two months.

3. My sister _____ a fever _____ last night.

4. Ali _____ allergies _____ he was five years old.

5. My feet have felt better _____ I saw the podiatrist.

6. I _____ dizzy _____ a couple of days now.

**I.** **Write present perfect sentences using** *for* **and** *since* **about yourself. Use the phrases given below.**

1. go to the same doctor _____

2. eat healthy _____

3. be sick _____

4. exercise _____

LESSON **3** **Health habits**

**GOAL** ■ Identify and analyze health habits

**A.** Every health habit has a certain effect. Think about the effects listed below and what might cause them. Write your ideas.

| Habit (cause) | Effect |
|---|---|
| *Go to bed late every night* | be tired |
| | have healthy lungs |
| | get skin cancer |
| | gain weight |
| | be fit |
| | be depressed |
| | have healthy skin |
| | have weak bones |
| | be hungry |
| | catch a cold |
| | stay healthy |

**B.** Look at the list of healthy and unhealthy habits in Exercise A and complete the table.

| Healthy habits | Unhealthy habits |
|---|---|
| | |

**C. Study the chart.**

| Future Conditional | |
|---|---|
| **Cause** | **Effect** |
| *If* + present tense | **Future tense** |
| *If* you *smoke,* | you *will have* unhealthy lungs |
| *If* they *don't exercise,* | they *will gain* weight. |
| *If* we *don't get* enough sleep, | we *will be* tired. |
| *If* I *run* every day, | I *will stay* in shape. |
| *If* he *doesn't get* enough calcium, | he *won't have* strong bones. |

- Use a future conditional statement to connect a cause and an effect.
- The *if*-clause (or the *cause*) is in the present tense and the *effect* clause is in the future tense.
- You can reverse the clauses, but use a comma only when the *if*-clause comes first.
  I will stay in shape **if** I run every day.
  **If** I run every day, I will stay in shape.

**D. Find the mistake in each sentence and correct it.**

1. She will develop diabetes if she ~~will eat~~ *eats* too much sugar.

2. Paulo will hurt his ankle if he will run too far.

3. Peter will gain weight if he will eat a large serving of food at every meal.

4. If you will become an obstetrician, you will work with mothers and babies.

5. If you exercise every day, it benefits your circulatory system.

6. If they eat enough fiber, they are healthy.

**E. Fill in the blank with the correct tense of the verb in parentheses.**

1. You (see) _____ a lot of children if you (become) _____ a pediatrician.

2. If he (run) _____ every day, he (develop) _____ endurance.

3. Jane (have) _____ difficulty running a marathon if she (have) _____ asthma.

4. His father (get) _____ an ulcer if he (worry) _____ too much.

5. If you (see) _____ a psychiatrist, he (ask) _____ why you are unhappy.

6. Her blood pressure (be) _____ too high if she (be) _____ not careful about her diet.

**F.** Make a list of your good health habits and bad health habits.

| Good habits | Bad habits |
| --- | --- |
| | |
| | |
| | |

**G.** Think about your health habits. What is the *effect* of each habit?

**Habit:** I walk every day.
**Effect:** I will stay in good shape.

**Habit:** I smoke.
**Effect:** I will have unhealthy lungs.

**Write down four of your health habits and the effects of those habits.**

1. Habit: _____

   Effect: _____

2. Habit: _____

   Effect: _____

3. Habit: _____

   Effect: _____

4. Habit: _____

   Effect: _____

**H.** Look at the good and bad health habits you wrote down in Exercise F. Write future conditional statements about those habits.

1. If I walk every day, I will stay in good shape. _____

2. _____

3. _____

4. _____

# LESSON ④ Nutrition labels

**GOAL** ■ Analyze nutrition information

**A.** **Think about giving health advice. Complete each piece of advice with the correct words by matching.**

1. You have a cold. Get _____.

2. Your bones are not strong. Eat _____.

3. You are too tense. Take _____.

4. You seem very nervous. _____.

5. You have a cavity. Brush _____.

6. You have heart problems. Don't eat _____.

7. If you want healthy lungs, don't _____.

8. Always stretch _____.

9. When you go out in the sun, put on _____.

10. Don't gain _____.

11. Avoid salt. Flavor _____.

12. You seem dehydrated. Drink some _____.

a. saturated fats

b. smoke

c. more calcium

d. after every meal

e. a vacation

f. weight

g. lots of sleep

h. your food with spices

i. Relax

j. after exercising

k. sunscreen

l. water

**B.** **Underline the verbs in the health advice above.**

**C.** **Using the words below, give nutrition advice.**

1. Eat _____.

2. Don't eat _____.

3. Drink _____.

4. Take _____.

5. Brush _____.

6. Put on _____.

**D. Study the chart.**

| Imperatives | | |
|---|---|---|
| **Imperative** | | |
| Take | this medication with water. | • Use imperatives to give instructions or warnings. |
| Don't take | it with a meal. | • A negative imperative is *do not (don't)* + base form. |
| Get | some rest. | • Do not use a subject. (*You* is understood.) |
| Do not stay | up too late. | |

**E. Respond with an appropriate imperative or negative imperative. Use the verbs in the box.**

| | | | |
|---|---|---|---|
| ~~eat~~ | keep | eat | stop |
| walk | sit | see | cook |

1. A: How can I eat better?

   B: ___Don't eat_____ high-fat foods.

3. A: Is exercise good for me?

   B: Yes. _____ regularly.

5. A: I want to stay healthy.

   B: _____ the doctor regularly.

7. A: I want to get some vitamins from my vegetables.

   B: _____ them too much.

2. A: My carrots never taste fresh.

   B: _____ them in the refrigerator.

4. A: I want to run faster.

   B: _____ smoking.

6. A: How can I avoid toothaches?

   B: _____ candy.

8. A: I feel dizzy.

   B: _____ down.

**F.  Lara has a few problems. Write the advice you would give her.**

Lara: I have a cavity.

Your advice: _____

Lara: I am always nervous.

Your advice: _____

Lara: I can't sleep at night.

Your advice: _____

Lara: I feel sick after I eat junk food.

Your advice: _____

**G.  Look back at the advice you gave Lara in Exercise F. Did you use imperatives?**

**H.  Think of some problems you have with your health.**

1. Problem: _____

2. Problem: _____

3. Problem: _____

4. Problem: _____

**I.  Write advice that you would give to yourself for each problem in Exercise H.**

1. Advice: _____

2. Advice: _____

3. Advice: _____

4. Advice: _____

# LESSON **5** Healthy living

---

**GOAL** ■ Interpret fitness information

**A.** Look at the list of activities below. Which ones do you do? Put a check (✓) in front of the ones you do at least once a week.

- ☐ walk
- ☐ run
- ☐ play soccer
- ☐ play basketball
- ☐ play golf
- ☐ clean the house
- ☐ ride a bike

- ☐ play with children
- ☐ walk up stairs
- ☐ ski
- ☐ dance
- ☐ go to the gym
- ☐ lift weights
- ☐ swim

**B.** Are there other activities you do that are not listed in Exercise A? Make a list on a separate piece of paper.

**C.** Match the statements below.

1. They play on a soccer team.
2. He skies in the winter.
3. The girls ride skateboards home from school.
4. Angelica walks to work.
5. His father does tai chi.
6. The older men swim in the ocean.

a. Do tai chi.
b. Walk to work.
c. Play on a soccer team.
d. Swim in the ocean.
e. Ski in the winter.
f. Ride skateboards home from school.

**D.** What is the difference between the matched statements above?

_____

_____

**E.  Study the chart.**

| Declarative Statements | |
|---|---|
| **Declarative statement** | |
| Shelley takes the stairs. | |
| Kimla plays in the park with her kids after school. | • A declarative statement is a sentence with a subject and a verb. |
| The guys play basketball during lunch. | |
| We don't eat fast food. | |

| Imperative Statements | |
|---|---|
| **Imperative statement** | |
| Take the stairs. | |
| Play in the park with your kids after school. | • An imperative statement gives advice or a warning and begins with a base verb. |
| Play basketball during lunch. | |
| Don't eat fast food. | |

**F.  Write *D* for declarative statements or *I* for imperative statements on each line below.**

1. Work in your garden.      __I__

2. Push the stroller.      _____

3. Clean the house.      _____

4. I clean my house once a week.      _____

5. John and Marla swim after work.      _____

6. We never eat dessert.      _____

7. Take a walk after dinner every night.      _____

8. Pick a sport and do it on the weekends.      _____

9. Drink eight glasses of water a day.      _____

10. I always stretch after I run.      _____

**G. Change each declarative statement into an imperative statement.**

1. They always go to the farmers' market.     _Always go to the farmers' market._

2. Our family eats small meals all day.     _____

3. Her sister goes to the gym before work.     _____

4. I don't eat junk food.     _____

5. We always stretch after we run.     _____

6. You ride your bike to school.     _____

7. We eat breakfast every morning.     _____

8. They take a walk after dinner.     _____

9. Their kids swim on a team.     _____

10. They play golf on vacation.     _____

**H. Look back at the list of activities in Exercises A and B. Think about people you know who do those activities and write declarative statements below.**

1. _Javier lifts weights._____

2. _____

3. _____

4. _____

5. _____

6. _____

7. _____

8. _____

# PRACTICE TEST

## A. Read the conversation and choose the best answers.

> **Doctor:** I have your test results back and the tests show that you have high blood pressure.
>
> **Scott:** We have a family history of high blood pressure and diabetes. I guess I'm glad it's high blood pressure. What should I do?
>
> **Doctor:** Well, the two things I recommend are blood pressure medication and changing your diet. I'll write up the prescription for the medication, and the nurse will talk you about how to start eating better.
>
> **Scott:** OK. Anything else?
>
> **Doctor:** That's it for now. But I'd like you to come back in a month to see how you're doing.
>
> **Scott:** Sounds good. Thank you doctor.

1. What did Scott's test results show?

   a. He has high blood pressure.          b. He has diabetes.

   c. He needs to eat healthier.           d. He needs a prescription.

2. What does Scott's doctor recommend?

   a. medication                           b. change in diet

   c. both A and B                         d. neither A nor B

## B. Read the situations and choose the best advice.

1. The boys are going to the beach.

   a. They should wear sunscreen.          b. They should stretch.

   c. They should take medication.         d. They should lose weight.

2. Marta's legs hurt the day after running.

   a. She should not smoke.                b. She should eat healthier.

   c. She should stretch after exercising. d. She should drink water.

**GOAL** ■ Identify job titles and skills

**A.** **Read the statements. What do you think each person's job is?**

| | | |
|---|---|---|
| dental hygienist | plumber | gardener |
| salesperson | nanny | nurse |
| ~~police officer~~ | firefighter | bus driver |
| mail carrier | technician | teacher |

1. I pull people over for speeding.     *police officer*

2. He works outside in people's yards. _____

3. She takes patients' temperatures. _____

4. He teaches children. _____

5. I deliver the mail. _____

6. I put out fires. _____

7. I clean teeth. _____

8. I fix leaking pipes. _____

9. She takes care of children. _____

10. I drive kids to school. _____

**B.** **Write three more job titles and describe what people with those jobs do.**

1. _____

2. _____

3. _____

**C.** **Underline the verb in each sentence in Exercise A. How are they all the same?**

**D. Study the chart.**

| Present Tense | | | |
|---|---|---|---|
| **Subject** | **Present tense** | | |
| I | file | papers. | • Use the present tense to describe what someone does at his or her job. <br> • For sentences with he, she, or it, use –**s** or –**es** at the end of the verb. |
| You | take | orders from customers. | |
| The custodian | clean**s** | the bathrooms. | |
| We | deliver | mail and packages. | |
| They | fix | leaking pipes. | |

**E. Check (✓) the answer next to the correct verb form for each sentence.**

1. We _____ houses.                    ☐ clean        ☐ cleans

2. He _____ a drill at a construction site.    ☐ operate      ☐ operates

3. She _____ computer programs.         ☐ write        ☐ writes

4. They _____ ads for food products.      ☐ design       ☐ designs

5. Kim _____ a camera for a TV show       ☐ operate      ☐ operates

6. He _____ people in court.              ☐ defend       ☐ defends

7. We _____ care of four children in our home.  ☐ take     ☐ takes

8. Jacob _____ broken air and heating units.   ☐ fix        ☐ fixes

9. She _____ a taxi from the airport.       ☐ drive        ☐ drives

10. We _____ airplane mechanics.          ☐ train        ☐ trains

11. His son _____ real estate.             ☐ sell         ☐ sells

12. My sister and I _____ in a gourmet restaurant.  ☐ cook    ☐ cooks

**F.** **Choose a verb from the box and write the correct form in each sentence below.**

| deliver | ~~design~~ | prepare | repair | sew | talk |
|---------|------------|---------|--------|-----|------|

1. We _____ design _____ advertisements for magazines.

2. He _____ computers that are broken.

3. She _____ dresses for a clothing company.

4. They _____ to customers.

5. He _____ pizza for the local pizza restaurant.

6. We _____ food in a Chinese restaurant.

**G.** **For each job title, write two things that person does.**

nurse

1. _A nurse takes temperatures._ _____

2. _____

mechanic

1. _____

2. _____

teacher

1. _____

2. _____

custodian

1. _____

2. _____

veterinarian

1. _____

2. _____

# LESSON ② What can you do?

GOAL ■ Identify job skills and personality traits

**A.** Think about your abilities related to employment. What do you like to do? What do you not like to do? Make a list and add two more to each column.

| answer phones | use a computer | clean | fix a car | make copies |
|---|---|---|---|---|
| sell a product | cook | drive a bus | teach | count money |

| Like | Dislike |
|---|---|
| | |

**B.** Make a list of what you like to do. Use *–ing* after the verb.

1. I like *answering* phones.

2. _____

3. _____

4. _____

5. _____

6. _____

## C. Study the chart.

| Gerunds and Infinitives | | | | | |
|---|---|---|---|---|---|
| Subject | Main verb | Infinitive or gerund | | Verb rule | Other verbs that follow the same rule |
| He | wants | *to get* | a job. | followed by an infinitive (*to* + verb) | plan, decide, agree, hope, learn, promise |
| She | enjoys | *fixing* | bicycles. | followed by a gerund (verb + *-ing*) | finish, give up, recommend, suggest |
| They | like | *walking.* *to walk.* | | followed by a gerund or an infinitive | love, hate, begin, continue, start |

## D. What follows each verb? Write *gerund* or *infinitive*. If either can be used, write *either*.

1. finish _____gerund_____      2. learn _____

3. love _____      4. plan _____

5. like _____      6. promise _____

7. give up _____      8. continue _____

9. decide _____      10. suggest _____

11. enjoy _____      12. start _____

13. agree _____      14. hate _____

15. recommend _____      16. begin _____

## E. Complete each phrase with a gerund or infinitive.

1. give up _____smoking_____      2. finish _____

3. learn _____      4. plan _____

5. promise _____      6. agree _____

**F.** **Complete each sentence with the correct form of the verb in parentheses. In some cases, two answers will be correct.**

1. We plan _____*to move*_____ (move) next year so my husband can be closer to his job.

2. She hopes _____ (get) a raise next month.

3. He finished _____ (work) on his job applications.

4. Hang loves _____ (be) at work late in the evenings.

5. Our manager agreed _____ (give) us a longer lunch break.

6. His friend suggested _____ (apply) for a job at the new restaurant down the street.

7. I start _____ (train) on Monday.

8. They continued _____ (organize) the stockroom.

**G.** **Write sentences about your likes, dislikes, and future goals related to employment.**

1. (want) *I want to apply for a new job next year.* _____

2. (plan) _____

3. (love) _____

4. (decide) _____

5. (enjoy) _____

6. (continue) _____

**H.** **Look back at what you wrote in Exercise B. Write sentences combining those ideas with verbs from Exercise G.**

1. *I like answering phones. I plan to look for a job as a customer service representative.* _____

2. _____
_____

3. _____
_____

4. _____
_____

LESSON **3** **Help wanted**

GOAL ■ Interpret job applications

**A.** **Choose one of the phrases from the box below to complete each sentence. More than one phrase is acceptable.**

| | | |
|---|---|---|
| living in the moment | asking for help | using the computer |
| learning about biology | selling houses | working with my hands |
| talking to customers | asking for a raise | working with other people |
| looking for a new job | | |

1. I am happy about _____.

2. They are good at _____.

3. She is interested in _____.

4. Their co-workers are worried about _____.

5. I am not so good at _____.

6. He has had experience in _____.

7. We would like training in _____.

8. They are not afraid of _____.

9. Her manager is excited about _____.

10. Jenna is known for _____.

**B.** **On a separate piece of paper, complete each sentence about yourself. Use the phrases from above and come up with your own ideas.**

**C. Study the chart.**

| Gerunds after Prepositions | | | | | |
|---|---|---|---|---|---|
| **Subject** | **Verb** | **Adjective** | **Preposition** | **Gerund / Noun** | |
| I | am | happy | about | getting | a new job. |
| She | is | good | at | fixing | machines. |
| They | are | interested | in | computers. | |
| He | is | afraid | of | not having | enough experience. |

**Rules**
- A gerund or a noun follows an adjective + preposition.
  Other examples of adjective + preposition are *tired of, bad at,* and *worried about.*
- To make the gerund negative, put *not* before the gerund.

**D. Complete each sentence with a gerund. Use the verbs in the box.**

| | | | | |
|---|---|---|---|---|
| train | use | lose | be | answer |
| make | learn | explain | finish | arrive |

1. Claude isn't good at _____ math questions.

2. We're tired of _____ new workers.

3. My boss is bad at _____ the benefits program.

4. She isn't good at _____ on time.

5. Lance is afraid of _____ his job.

6. We are happy about not _____ laid off.

7. They are worried about _____ decisions.

8. I am interested in _____ about new cooking styles.

9. She is afraid of _____ that new machine.

10. They are good at _____ their work on time.

**E.   Write a new sentence using adjective + preposition + gerund.**

1. She writes letters very well.

   _____

2. Learning new skills makes him happy.

   _____

3. He may become a landscaper. That's his newest interest.

   _____

4. Ramona doesn't want to lose her job. She is worried.

   _____

5. She doesn't know how to operate machines.

   _____

6. I'm tired. I don't want to explain my decision.

   _____

7. She doesn't like to use electric tools. She's afraid of them.

   _____

8. Eric likes to talk to customers.

   _____

**F.   Imagine you are being interviewed. How would you answer the following questions?**

1. What are you good at?

   _____

2. What are you interested in?

   _____

3. What are you not so good at?

   _____

4. What are you afraid of?

   _____

# LESSON **4** Employment history

**GOAL** ■ Complete a job application

**A.** Look at the list of items below and circle the ones you would find on a job application.

| | |
|---|---|
| education | parents' names |
| availability | weight |
| employment history | name |
| address | phone number |
| reason for leaving last job | job |
| signature | age |
| expected salary | type of car you drive |

**B.** Sandra and Kyung are both looking for jobs. Read about them.

| Sandra | Kyung |
|---|---|
| • She used to work for a computer company. | • He is used to waking up in the afternoon to go to work. |
| • She used to take orders over the phone. | • He is used to studying before he goes to work. |
| • She used to work full-time. | • He is used to cooking dinner before he leaves for work. |
| • She used to go to school at night. | • He is used to working the night shift. |

**C.** Notice the two different forms of *used to.* What do you think the difference in meaning is?

_____

_____

## D. Study the chart.

| Used to | |
|---|---|
| **Example** | **Explanation** |
| I used to work for Data Computers. | *Used to* + base form describes a repeated action in the past or a situation that existed in the past. |
| I used to train employees. | |
| I am used to working with computers. | *Be used to* + gerund describes an action or a situation that has become familiar. |
| I am used to troubleshooting. | |

## E. Circle *past* if the sentence talks about a situation in the past and *familiar* if it talks about a situation that has become familiar.

1. My family is used to working.                   past        familiar

2. My mother used to be a nurse.                   past        familiar

3. She is used to taking care of people.           past        familiar

4. She used to work in a large hospital.           past        familiar

5. My father used to work as a security guard.     past        familiar

6. He used to work the night shift.                past        familiar

7. He is used to sleeping during the day.          past        familiar

8. My parents used to work very hard.              past        familiar

9. Now they are used to being retired.             past        familiar

10. I am used to working long hours.               past        familiar

**F. Complete each sentence using either the base or the gerund form of the verb in parentheses.**

1. I used to _____ (eat) lunch with my coworkers.

2. I used to _____ (work) in an office. Now I work at home.

3. I used to _____ (wake up) at 7:00. Now I can wake up later.

4. I am so used to _____ (wake up) at 7:00 that I can't sleep later.

5. I used to _____ (take) the subway every morning. Now I never take the subway.

6. I am used to _____ (hear) phones ringing. It's strange to be in a quiet home.

7. I am used to _____ (see) many people during the day. It's a little lonely at home.

8. I used to _____ (wear) a dress every day. Now I wear jeans.

**G. Write two sentences about things you used to do in the past.**

1. _____

2. _____

**H. Write two sentences about things you are used to.**

1. _____

2. _____

**I. Put a check mark (✓) next to the things you *don't* want to say in an interview.**

☐ I am used to showing up late for work.

☐ I am used to working hard.

☐ I used to train machine operators.

☐ I used to take two-hour lunch breaks.

☐ I am used to wearing flip-flops to work.

☐ I used to take paper home from the copy room.

# L E S S O N **5** Why do you want to work here?

**GOAL** ■ Interview for a job

**A.** Think about your skills and abilities. Write an adjective in front of each noun to describe yourself.

1. _____ hard _____ worker

2. _____ learner

3. _____ speaker

4. _____ student

5. _____ employee

6. _____ family member

| **Example Adjectives** | |
|---|---|
| fast | quick |
| slow | outstanding |
| smart | brave |
| caring | lazy |
| enthusiastic | fun |
| good | great |
| bad | hard |

**B.** Look at the box of example adjectives. Which ones are positive (things you would say about yourself in a job interview) and which ones are negative? Complete the table and then add some adjectives of your own.

| Positive adjectives | Negative adjectives |
|---|---|
| fast | |

**C.** Think about your ideal job situation. What are your preferences? Choose one from each of the questions below.

1. Would you rather work for a large company or a small company?

   ☐ large company          ☐ small company

2. Would you rather work alone or with other people?

   ☐ work alone          ☐ work with other people

3. Would you rather work for a manager or be a manager?

   ☐ work for a manager          ☐ be a manager

4. Would you rather work part-time or full-time?

   ☐ work part-time          ☐ work full-time

5. Would you rather make more money or have four weeks paid vacation per year?

   ☐ make more money          ☐ have four weeks paid vacation

**D. Study the chart.**

| | | | | | | |
|---|---|---|---|---|---|---|
| | | | *Would Rather* | | | |
| | *Would* | Subject | *Rather* | Base form | *Or* | Base form |
| Questions | Would | Kim | **rather** | file | or | answer phones? |
| | Would | you | **rather** | work days | or | (work) nights? |
| | Subject | *Would rather* | | Base form | *Than* | Base form |
| Statements | She | **would rather** | | answer phones | than | type. |
| | I | **'d rather** | | work days | than | nights. |

**Rules**
- *Or* is used between the choices in a question.
- *Than* is used between the choices in a statement.
- The second verb in questions and statements can be omitted if it is the same as the first.
- *Would* is often contracted in statements: **I'd, you'd, he'd, she'd, we'd, they'd.**

**E. Unscramble the words to make questions and statements with *would rather*.**

1. (question) in  /  an  /  office / in / a / school / you / rather / work / or / would

_____

2. (statement) take / a / class / study / at / home / than / she'd / rather

_____

3. (statement) use / computers / repair / computers / they'd / than / rather

_____

4. (question) balance / accounts / talk / to / customers / or / she / rather / would

_____

5. (question) rather / he / would / join / a / work / alone / team / or

_____

6. (question) would / home / to / an / office / or / work / go / rather / you / from

_____

**F.   Write questions using *would rather* and the words below.**

1. work inside / work outside

   <u>Would you rather work inside or outside?</u>

2. work days / nights

   _____

3. retire at 65 / work until you are 70

   _____

4. get paid hourly / weekly

   _____


**G.   Answer each of the questions above for yourself. Give a reason for your answer.**

1. <u>I would rather work outside because I love the fresh air.</u>

2. _____

3. _____

4. _____


**H.   Look back at how you described yourself in Exercise A. Write sentences you would use in a job interview.**

1. <u>I am a quick learner. I learn new things quickly.</u>

2. _____

3. _____

4. _____

5. _____

6. _____

**A.   Read and choose the best answer.**

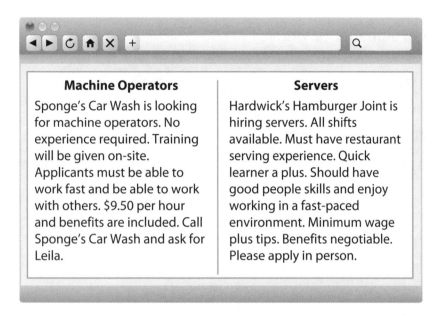

**Machine Operators**

Sponge's Car Wash is looking for machine operators. No experience required. Training will be given on-site. Applicants must be able to work fast and be able to work with others. $9.50 per hour and benefits are included. Call Sponge's Car Wash and ask for Leila.

**Servers**

Hardwick's Hamburger Joint is hiring servers. All shifts available. Must have restaurant serving experience. Quick learner a plus. Should have good people skills and enjoy working in a fast-paced environment. Minimum wage plus tips. Benefits negotiable. Please apply in person.

1. Which position is Hardwick's Hamburger Joint advertising?

   a. a fast-paced environment

   b. benefits

   c. a server position in a restaurant

   d. a manager at Hardwick's Hamburger Joint

2. What skills does Sponge's Car Wash require?

   a. a server

   b. a quick learner

   c. a fast-paced environment

   d. someone who works well with others

3. What is the pay at Hardwick's Hamburger Joint?

   a. tips

   b. minimum wage plus tips

   c. minimum wage

   d. minimum wage, tips, and benefits

4. How do you apply for the job at Sponge's Car Wash?

   a. fill out an application

   b. apply online

   c. call

   d. go into the restaurant and ask the manager

# LESSON ① Attitudes at work

**GOAL** ■ Compare employee attitudes and behavior

**A.** Put the following words in alphabetical order.

| | | | | |
|---|---|---|---|---|
| relaxed | motivated | friendly | courteous | lazy |
| efficient | respectful | demanding | patient | quiet |
| strict | intelligent | reserved | interesting | funny |
| disorganized | easygoing | hardworking | opinionated | impatient |

1. _____    2. _____

3. _____    4. _____

5. _____    6. _____

7. _____    8. _____

9. _____    10. _____

11. _____   12. _____

13. _____   14. _____

15. _____   16. _____

17. _____   18. _____

19. _____   20. _____

**B.** Look at the words in Exercise A. Which ones are positive and which ones are negative? Which ones could be both positive and negative? Complete the Venn diagram with the numbers from Exercise A.

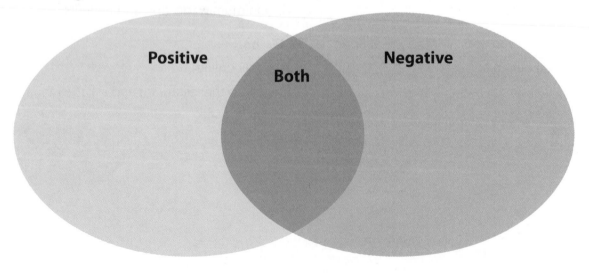

**C.** Which words would you use to describe your co-workers? Which words would you use to describe your boss?

| Co-workers | Boss |
|---|---|
|  |  |

**D.** Read the conversation between Leticia and Ellen.

**Leticia:** So how is *your* new job?

**Ellen:** It's pretty good. Although *my* boss is quite demanding and she always wants *her* reports before they are due. It seems like she thinks *her* time is more important than **ours**.

**Leticia:** Really? It sounds like *your* manager is harder to work with than **mine**. *My* manager is really friendly because she wants *her* staff to work hard for her.

**Ellen:** **Yours** sounds like a pleasure to work for compared to **mine**. Are they hiring at *your* company?

**E.** Look at all the words in *italics* and **bold**. Make two lists below.

| Italics | Bold |
|---|---|
| *your* | ours |

**F.** Which words in Exercise E are adjectives and which ones are pronouns? Study the chart.

| Possessive Adjectives and Possessive Pronouns | | | |
|---|---|---|---|
|  | Possessive | Example | Explanation |
| Adjectives | my, your, his, her, our, their | My pay is $500 a week. | Possessive adjectives come before a noun and show possession. |
| Pronouns | mine, yours, his, hers, ours, theirs | Yours is $450 a week. | Possessive pronouns take the place of a noun and show possession. |
| **Rule** A noun never comes after a possessive pronoun: *Mine office is clean.* | | | |

## G. Circle the correct possessive form.

1. She works the day shift. (Her/Hers) hours are 9:00 a.m. to 5:00 p.m.

2. My net pay is $1,200. (Her/Hers) is $1,000.

3. His paycheck was late. (My/Mine) was on time.

4. My tax deductions are very high, but (your/yours) aren't.

5. Their company pays for disability insurance, but (my/mine) company doesn't.

6. They didn't give me my paycheck yet. Did you get (your/yours) check?

## H. Use a possessive adjective or a possessive pronoun to rewrite each second sentence. Use the correct form of *Be* where necessary.

1. My pay is $7.50 an hour. How much do you make?

   (possessive pronoun) _How much is yours?_

2. My deductions are over 30% of my pay. How much do you pay?

   (possessive adjective) _____

3. Fred makes about $400 a month. Fred's sister makes about $900 a month.

   (possessive adjective) _____

4. So's company pays for Medicare. The company I work for doesn't pay for it.

   (possessive pronoun) _____

5. Susan's co-workers are friendly. The people I work with aren't.

   (possessive pronoun) _____

6. Alexander's net pay goes up every year. The amount you get paid doesn't go up.

   (possessive adjective) _____

## I. Write sentences about your job using the words in parentheses below (note: your job might be a student or a homemaker).

1. (her, mine) _Her job is easier than mine._

2. (his, theirs) _____

3. (their, ours) _____

4. (your, hers) _____

# LESSON **2** It's pay day!

**GOAL** ■ Interpret a pay stub

## A. Write the nouns in the correct column. Make the count nouns plural.

| ~~money~~ | earnings | pay | deduction | employee |
|---|---|---|---|---|
| ~~hour~~ | job | time | knowledge | manager |

**Count Nouns**

hours  _____  _____

_____  _____

_____  _____

_____  _____

**Non-Count Nouns**

money  _____

_____  _____

_____  _____

_____  _____

## B. Look at Karl's pay stub and answer the questions.

| Hours and Earnings | | | |
|---|---|---|---|
| | Rate of Pay | Hours/Units | Earnings |
| Hourly | $12.25 | 80 | $980.00 |

| Pre-Tax Deductions | |
|---|---|
| Description | Amount |
| 401K | $45.00 |
| Current Total | $45.00 |
| Year-to-Date Total | $360.00 |

| | Gross Pay | Pre-Tax Deductions | Tax Deductions | Net Pay |
|---|---|---|---|---|
| Current | $980.00 | $45.00 | $75.62 | |

1. How many hours did he work in the past two weeks?  _____

2. How much does he get paid?  _____

3. How much does he contribute to his 401K?  _____

4. How much money did he make this month after taxes?  _____

(Hint: Take the gross pay and subtract the two deductions.)

5. How much money did he make before taxes?  _____

## C. Study the chart.

| How Much and How Many | | | |
|---|---|---|---|
| *How many* | **Count noun** | | **Rule** |
| **How many** | deductions | does Fred have? | Use *How many* questions to ask about things that can be counted. |
| **How many** | sick days | did Ellen use last year? | |
| *How much* | **Non-Count noun** | | **Rule** |
| **How much** | tax | does Fred pay? | Use *How much* questions to ask about things that can't be counted. |
| **How much** | vacation | did Ellen take last year? | |

## D. Write the questions using words and phrases from each column.

| A | B | C |
|---|---|---|
| How many<br>How much | English<br>programs<br>state tax<br>sick days<br>experience<br>overtime<br>money<br>meal tickets<br>time | did you pay this month<br>are you willing to work each week<br>did you take when you broke your leg<br>do we spend on office supplies every year<br>do we have before the meeting<br>have you studied<br>do you need before you get a promotion<br>do you need for your co-workers<br>can you run on this computer |

1. _How much English have you studied?_

2. _____

3. _____

4. _____

5. _____

6. _____

7. _____

8. _____

9. _____

**E.** **Think about your ideal job and answer the questions below.**

1. How much money do you want to make? _____

2. How many hours a week do you want to work? _____

3. How many days a week do you want to work? _____

4. How much vacation time do you want? _____

5. How many employees do you want to work with? _____

6. How many miles from work do you want to live? _____

7. How much experience do you want your manager to have? _____

**F.** **Write *How much* and *How many* questions using six of the words in the box below.**

| sick days | hours | money |
|-----------|-------|-------|
| insurance | employees | overtime |
| days | vacation | breaks |

1. **Question:** _How many sick days do you get?_

   **Answer:** _I get 10 sick days per year._

2. **Q:** _____

   **A:** _____

3. **Q:** _____

   **A:** _____

4. **Q:** _____

   **A:** _____

5. **Q:** _____

   **A:** _____

6. **Q:** _____

   **A:** _____

# LESSON **3** What are the benefits?

**GOAL** ■ Analyze benefit information

**A. Read the benefits Company A and Company B offer.**

| Benefits at Company A | Benefits at Company B |
| --- | --- |
| paid sick days | paid vacation |
| maternity leave | paid personal days |
| health insurance | maternity and paternity leave |
| bonuses | dental insurance |
| overtime | 401K |
| life insurance | daycare |

**B. Which company in Exercise A do you prefer and why?**

_____

_____

_____

_____

**C. Choose the five most important benefits to you. Write them in order from most important to least important.**

1. _____

2. _____

3. _____

4. _____

5. _____

**D. Study the chart.**

| Prefer ... to | | | | | |
|---|---|---|---|---|---|
| Subject | *Prefer* | Noun | *to* | Noun | |
| I | prefer | eye-care benefits | to | dental benefits. | • Use *prefer* to give your preferences. |
| She | prefers | time off | to | overtime. | |
| He | prefers | working | to | studying. | • Use *to* between the two nouns. |
| They | prefer | paid vacation | to | paid personal days. | |

**E. Correct the mistake in each sentence below.**

1. She ~~prefer~~ prefers her old job to her new job.

2. The guys prefers dental insurance to maternity leave.

3. She prefer overtime to daycare.

4. I prefers the benefits at my old job to the benefits at my new job.

5. We prefer be part of a small company to working for a large one.

6. Joanne prefer her new boss to her old one.

7. You prefer working part-time or working full-time, don't you?

8. He prefer driving to work to walking to work.

9. We prefers weekly pay to monthly pay.

10. I prefer holidays than working overtime.

11. They prefers a 401K to bonuses.

12. He prefers chiropractic benefits acupuncture benefits.

**F.** **Choose a subject and two nouns to write sentences below.**

| Subject | Noun | Noun |
|---|---|---|
| I | bonuses | leaving early |
| We | female bosses | overtime |
| They | ~~life insurance~~ | earning minimum wage |
| She | skipping lunch | male bosses |
| Rick and Georgia | taking breaks | owning their own business |
| ~~The girls~~ | working for someone else | ~~paid vacation~~ |
| My co-worker and I | earning tips | staying late |

1. *The girls prefer life insurance to paid vacation.* _____

2. _____

3. _____

4. _____

5. _____

6. _____

**G.** **What are your benefit preferences? Write five sentences below using the ideas you wrote in Exercise C.**

1. _____

_____

2. _____

_____

3. _____

_____

4. _____

_____

5. _____

_____

# LESSON ④ Workplace safety

**GOAL** ■ Identify safe workplace behavior

## A. Read Fred and Arnie's conversation.

**Fred:** Arnie, why aren't you wearing a back support belt?

**Arnie:** Oh, I don't need one.

**Fred:** If you don't wear a belt, you might get hurt.

**Arnie:** I don't think so. I'm really careful.

**Fred:** I know, but you could fall. Or you might lift something that is too heavy.

**Arnie:** You're right. If I get hurt, I might miss work. I could lose a lot of money if I can't work.

**Fred:** Exactly. Let me get you a belt.

## B. Answer the questions.

1. Why does Fred want Arnie to wear a back support belt?

   _____

2. Why does Arnie think he doesn't need one?

   _____

3. What would happen if Arnie gets hurt?

   _____

4. Who gets Arnie the belt?

   _____

5. Do you think Arnie puts the belt on? Why or why not?

   _____

## C. Underline the words *could* and *might* in the conversation in Exercise A. What do you think these words mean?

**D. Study the chart.**

| Modals *Could* and *Might* | | | | |
|---|---|---|---|---|
| **Subject** | **Modal** | **Base verb** | | |
| I<br>You<br>He<br>She<br>It<br>We<br>They | could | fall<br>get<br>lose | off the ladder.<br>hurt.<br>a lot of money. | We use the modals *might* and *could* to say that there is a chance that something will happen in the future. |
| | might | miss | work. | |

**E. Correct the mistake in each sentence below.**

          start

1. You might ~~starts~~ a fire if you don't put out that cigarette.

2. She could falls off the scaffolding if she isn't careful.

3. The cook could got hair in the food if he doesn't wear a hairnet.

4. The machine operator could losing his eyesight if he doesn't wear safety goggles.

5. He might threw his back out if he doesn't wear his safety belt.

6. There might is a fire if you have too many cords plugged into one outlet.

**F. Use a verb from the box with *could* or *might* to complete each sentence.**

| lose | fall | ~~slip~~ | quit | hurt | miss |
|---|---|---|---|---|---|

1. They _could slip_____ if they don't clean up the spill on the floor.

2. He _____ if he climbs onto the top step of the ladder.

3. We _____ our hearing if we don't wear earplugs around the loud machinery.

4. Jenna _____ her back if she doesn't wear a back support belt.

5. I _____ my job if I can't get more hours.

6. You _____ work if you slip and fall.

**G. Complete each sentence using *could* or *might*.**

1. If he doesn't wear a helmet, _____.

2. If she doesn't wear her work boots, _____.

3. _____ if they don't wear hairnets.

4. If they don't wear earplugs, _____.

5. If they don't walk slowly, _____.

6. _____ if she doesn't wear her safety goggles.

7. _____ if he doesn't wear his safety belt.

8. If he doesn't clean up the spill, _____.

**H. Identify the six safety items in Exercise G. Make a list.**

1. _____

2. _____

3. _____

4. _____

5. _____

6. _____

**I. Using each item listed in Exercise H, write a warning statement.**

1. *If you don't wear ear plugs, you could lose your hearing.*

2. _____

3. _____

4. _____

5. _____

6. _____

# LESSON **5** Good job!

---

**GOAL** ■ Communicate at work

## A. Write *criticism* or *compliment* next to each statement.

1. Your training on how to put on the safety gear was excellent!  _____

2. You shouldn't be sitting in the restaurant during your break.  _____

3. Your presentation was clear and easy to understand.  _____

4. Please don't text during your shift.  _____

5. Your design was innovative and the customer loved it!  _____

6. This is your final warning about taking long breaks.  _____

7. You handled that customer complaint very well.  _____

8. You need to work faster if you are going to get all the reports filed.  _____

## B. Read the conversations. How are the conversations the same? How are they different? Answer the questions that follow.

Two Friends:

**Friend #1:** Can you help me pick out something to wear this weekend?

**Friend #2:** Sure.

Two Employees:

**Employee:** Would you mind helping me with these reports?

**Employee:** Yes, of course.

1. What question words do the friends use?

   _____

2. What question words do the employees use?

   _____

3. What is the difference between *can* and *would*?

   _____

**C. Study the chart.**

| Polite Requests: *Would you mind . . .* and *Could you . . . ?* | |
|---|---|
| **Request** | **Description** |
| **Would you mind** making a copy for me? | polite and formal |
| **Could you look** over this report? | polite and less formal |
| **Can you help** me with this box? | polite and informal |
| Give me that! | very informal or impolite |
| **Rules**<br>• *Would you mind* is followed by a gerund.<br>• *Can* and *could* are followed by the base form.<br>• Use polite and formal language when talking with a boss or manager.<br>• Use polite or informal language when talking with co-workers.<br>• Use very informal or impolite language in an emergency or to show anger. | |

**D. Label each request. Use the descriptions above.**

1. Can you answer the phone?                                           _polite and informal_

2. Can you help me with these reports?                         _____

3. Call the boss right away!                                             _____

4. Can you come in early tomorrow morning?             _____

5. Would you mind changing your appointment?         _____

6. Would you mind reviewing my resume again?          _____

7. Could you sign all three copies?                                 _____

**E. Look at the descriptions and write requests.**

1. (polite and formal) _____

2. (polite and less formal) _____

3. (polite and informal) _____

4. (very informal and impolite) _____

**F. Complete the responses. Some answers can use either *can* or *could*.**

1. (lend me your goggles) To a friend:

   *Hey, Ellen! Can you lend me your goggles?* _____

2. (sign this check) To your supervisor:

   Oh, Ms. Reeves. _____, please?

3. (open the door) To a friend:

   Say, José. _____ for me?

4. (help me pick them up) To a stranger:

   Oh, no! I dropped all the reports. _____

5. (answer the phones) To your co-worker:

   Oh, Arnie. _____ while I'm at lunch?

6. (open the door) To a friend:

   I'm in a hurry! _____

7. (check this report) To your manager:

   I know you're busy, Mr. Adams, but _____?

8. (sign these letters) To your company president:

   Excuse me, Mrs. Camus. _____?


**G. Imagine you are having conversations based on the situations below. Write a request.**

Situation #1: You want to borrow a classmate's pencil.

Request: _____

Situation #2: You want the teacher to help you after class.

Request: _____

Situation #3: You want your children to clean their rooms.

Request: _____

Situation #4: You want to talk to your boss about a raise.

Request: _____

# PRACTICE TEST

## A. Read and choose the best answer.

### Benefits: Sick Days and Vacation Days

All employees have 10 paid sick days per year. You will not be paid for any other sick days. After each month of working, you will acquire one paid vacation day, so at the end of 12 months, you will have 12 paid vacation days. Vacation days do roll over for up to three years. If you do not use the vacation days within the three-year period, you will lose the days but receive the pay in your paycheck.

1. How many sick days are allowed per year?

    a. 10                              b. 12

    c. 1 day for each month of work      d. It doesn't say.

2. How many paid sick days are given per year?

    a. 10                              b. 12

    c. 1 day for each month of work      d. It doesn't say.

3. What happens if you don't use your vacation days within three years?

    a. You lose them.                 b. You get paid for them.

    c. a and b                      d. neither a nor b

4. What if you need more than ten sick days per year?

    a. You can't have more than 10.      b. You can take more sick days, but you won't get paid.

    c. You can take more sick days, but you only get paid half your salary.      d. You can exchange your sick days for vacation days.

5. At the end of one year, how many combined sick and vacation days can you have (if you don't use any of them)?

    a. 10                              b. 12

    c. 20                            d. 22

# LESSON **1** The United States

---

**GOAL** ■ Identify U.S. geographical locations

## A. Which states do these abbreviations represent?

1. NH _____     2. OK _____

3. MS _____     4. CT _____

5. TN _____     6. WA _____

7. NE _____     8. RI _____

9. VA _____     10. AL _____

## B. Which states have you lived in or visited? Which ones do you want to visit? Check (✔) the correct columns.

| State | Lived in/ visited | Want to live in or visit | State | Lived in/ visited | Want to live in or visit | State | Lived in/ visited | Want to live in or visit |
|---|---|---|---|---|---|---|---|---|
| Alabama | ☐ | ☐ | Kentucky | ☐ | ☐ | North Carolina | ☐ | ☐ |
| Alaska | ☐ | ☐ | Louisiana | ☐ | ☐ | North Dakota | ☐ | ☐ |
| Arizona | ☐ | ☐ | Maine | ☐ | ☐ | Ohio | ☐ | ☐ |
| Arkansas | ☐ | ☐ | Maryland | ☐ | ☐ | Oklahoma | ☐ | ☐ |
| California | ☐ | ☐ | Massachusetts | ☐ | ☐ | Oregon | ☐ | ☐ |
| Colorado | ☐ | ☐ | Michigan | ☐ | ☐ | Pennsylvania | ☐ | ☐ |
| Connecticut | ☐ | ☐ | Minnesota | ☐ | ☐ | Rhode Island | ☐ | ☐ |
| Delaware | ☐ | ☐ | Mississippi | ☐ | ☐ | South Carolina | ☐ | ☐ |
| Florida | ☐ | ☐ | Missouri | ☐ | ☐ | South Dakota | ☐ | ☐ |
| Georgia | ☐ | ☐ | Montana | ☐ | ☐ | Tennessee | ☐ | ☐ |
| Hawaii | ☐ | ☐ | Nebraska | ☐ | ☐ | Texas | ☐ | ☐ |
| Idaho | ☐ | ☐ | Nevada | ☐ | ☐ | Utah | ☐ | ☐ |
| Illinois | ☐ | ☐ | New Hampshire | ☐ | ☐ | Vermont | ☐ | ☐ |
| Indiana | ☐ | ☐ | New Jersey | ☐ | ☐ | Virginia | ☐ | ☐ |
| Iowa | ☐ | ☐ | New Mexico | ☐ | ☐ | Washington | ☐ | ☐ |
| Kansas | ☐ | ☐ | New York | ☐ | ☐ | West Virginia | ☐ | ☐ |
| | | | | | | Wisconsin | ☐ | ☐ |
| | | | | | | Wyoming | ☐ | ☐ |

**C. Study the chart.**

| *But* and *However* | | |
| --- | --- | --- |
| **First idea** | **Second idea** | **Statement of contrast** |
| California is on the West Coast. | New Jersey isn't on the West Coast. | California is on the West Coast, but New Jersey isn't. |
| Texas produces a lot of oil. | Kentucky doesn't produce a lot of oil. | Texas produces a lot of oil; however, Kentucky doesn't. |
| **Rules** | | |
| • Use a comma before a contrasting statement that starts with *but*.<br>• Use a semicolon before a contrasting statement that starts with *however* and use a comma after the word *however*.<br>• Use a subject and helping verb in the contrasting statement.<br>  California is on the West Coast, but New Jersey isn't. ~~on the West coast~~<br>  Texas produces a lot of oil; however, Kentucky doesn't. ~~produce a lot of oil.~~ | | |

**D. Match the two parts of each sentence.**

1. Puc and his wife went to Florida;              a. but his sister doesn't.

2. New Jersey is in the East;                     b. however, Oregon isn't.

3. Texas is a very large state,                   c. however, Mindy hasn't.

4. San Francisco is in California,                d. but Rhode Island isn't.

5. Abdullah wants to visit Oklahoma,              e. however, their kids didn't.

6. Lim has lived in South Dakota,                 f. however, his wife doesn't.

7. The boys want to move to Chicago,              g. but their parents don't.

8. Judy has visited Kentucky;                     h. but Houston isn't.

9. Paul wants to move to Michigan;                i. but Jasmine hasn't.

**E. Write complete sentences using the ideas in Exercise D.**

1. Puc and his wife went to Florida; however, their kids didn't.

2. _____

3. _____

4. _____

**F. Use the words to write contrasts with *but* and *however*.**

1. Liz has visited Texas. Ali hasn't visited Texas.

   (but) Liz has visited Texas, but Ali hasn't. _____

2. The Statue of Liberty is in New York. The Liberty Bell isn't in New York.

   (however) _____

3. Texas is a big oil producer. Kentucky isn't a big oil producer.

   (but) _____

4. San Francisco is a major port. Hollywood isn't a major port.

   (however) _____

5. Massachusetts was a British colony. Oklahoma wasn't a British colony.

   (but) _____

6. Abraham Lincoln was assassinated. George Washington wasn't assassinated.

   (but) _____

7. Labor Day is in September. Veteran's Day is not in September.

   (however) _____

**G. Look back at Exercise B. Write sentences about yourself and people you know.**

1. I have lived in Idaho, but my cousin Mary hasn't. _____

2. _____

3. _____

4. _____

5. _____

6. _____

# LESSON **2** Which party?

**GOAL** ■ Compare and contrast ideas

## A. Think about the following issues. Do you agree or disagree?

| | | |
|---|---|---|
| 1. We should raise taxes to build more parks. | agree | disagree |
| 2. We should offer job training for homeless people. | agree | disagree |
| 3. We should increase the number of police officers. | agree | disagree |
| 4. We should raise tuition for immigrant students. | agree | disagree |
| 5. We should raise taxes to improve the libraries. | agree | disagree |

## B. Look at the chart about the citizens. Write *True* or *False* after each statement.

| | Rosario | Cherie | Jackson | Suzanna |
|---|---|---|---|---|
| **Voted** | no | no | yes | no |
| **Marches in parades** | no | yes | yes | yes |
| **Has met the mayor** | no | no | yes | no |

1. Both Rosario and Cherie voted. _____*False*_____

2. Neither Rosario nor Cherie has met the mayor. _____

3. Both Jackson and Suzanna march in parades. _____

4. Both Rosario and Cherie march in parades. _____

5. Neither Cherie nor Suzanna has met the mayor. _____

6. Neither Suzanna nor Jackson voted. _____

7. Both Jackson and Cherie have met the mayor. _____

8. Neither Suzanna nor Cherie voted. _____

## C. Study the chart.

| Both and Neither | | |
|---|---|---|
| **First idea** | **Second idea** | **Statement of agreement** |
| Enrico wants to lower class sizes in elementary schools. | Ali wants to lower class sizes in elementary schools. | **Both** Enrico **and** Ali want to lower class sizes in elementary schools. |
| Enrico doesn't want high taxes. | Ali doesn't want high taxes. | **Neither** Enrico **nor** Ali wants high taxes. |

**Rules**
- Use *and* in statements beginning with *both*.
- Use *nor* in statements beginning with *neither*.
- In a *both/and* statement, the verb agrees with the combined subject.
    *Both* Maria *and* Marco **are** citizens.
- In a *neither/nor* statement, the verb agrees with the second subject.
    *Neither* Maria *nor* Marco **is** a citizen.

## D. Correct the error(s) in each sentence.

1. Both the secretary of state ~~nor~~ and the secretary of defense ~~is~~ are in the cabinet.

2. Neither the executive and judicial branch can make laws.

3. Both the president and the vice president lives in Washington, D.C.

4. Neither the House of Representatives nor the Senate have 600 members.

5. Neither the president nor the cabinet are part of the judicial branch.

6. Both the Senate and the House of Representatives is part of Congress.

7. Neither the executive branch and the legislative branch control immigration.

8. Both Texas and Rhode Island has two senators.

**E. Complete each statement with *both* or *neither*.**

1. _____ Alex and Kim want to build more public schools.

2. _____ the outgoing mayor and the new candidate want to improve library facilities.

3. _____ Maria nor Eliza want to raise taxes.

4. _____ Mr. Sanchez nor Miss Truong want to raise the tuition.

5. _____ the governor and the mayor want to hire more firefighters.

6. _____ the president nor the senate want to increase healthcare costs.

7. _____ the business owners and the residents want to reduce traffic.

8. _____ Manjiri and Sam want to put in more stoplights.

**F. Read the table and write sentences comparing Luke and Scott.**

|  | U.S. citizens | Library cards | Students | Pay taxes | Own a house |
|---|---|---|---|---|---|
| Scott | yes | no | yes | yes | no |
| Luke | yes | no | yes | yes | no |

1. Both Luke and Scott are U.S. citizens. _____

2. _____

3. _____

4. _____

5. _____

# LESSON **3** U.S. government

**GOAL** ■ Interpret the branches of U.S. government

## A. Read what the city officers have to say about their jobs.

**Jim:** I'm the <u>tax assessor</u>. I help set tax rates by deciding the value of property.

**Su Young:** I'm the <u>city clerk</u>, and I keep track of records of property, local businesses, and registered voters. I also issue birth certificates and marriage licenses.

**Christopher:** I'm a <u>city council member</u>. I help represent this community. All the council members meet with the mayor to discuss and solve community problems.

**Sheryl:** I'm the <u>superintendent of schools</u>. I oversee the county schools and help them do their job in providing a good education to our children.

**Matt:** I'm the <u>mayor</u> of this town. I'm the head of the city government, and I work with all the city council members to keep our community strong and happy.

## B. Complete each sentence with the correct job title.

1. The schools are overseen by the _____.

2. The community is represented by the _____.

3. Property records are kept by the _____.

4. Birth certificates are issued by the _____.

5. Property values are decided by the _____.

## C. Rewrite the sentences above.

1. The superintendent oversees the schools.

2. _____

3. _____

4. _____

5. _____

**D. Study the chart.**

| Active and Passive Voices | |
|---|---|
| **Active voice** | **Passive voice (*be* + past participle)** |
| The city clerk issues marriage licenses. | Marriage licenses are issued by the city clerk. |
| The city council members represent the citizens. | The citizens are represented by the city council members. |

**Rules**
• The active voice shows that the subject of the sentence performs the action.
• The passive voice shows that the subject of the sentence receives the action.
• *Be* in a passive sentence is in the same tense as the verb in the active sentence.

**E. Decide if each sentence is active or passive. Write *active* or *passive* on the line.**

1. The justices are selected by the president and Congress. _____*passive*_____

2. The president commands the military. _____

3. Congress makes the laws. _____

4. The U.S. government was set up with three branches. _____

5. The cabinet advises the president. _____

6. The justices of the Supreme Court make legal judgments. _____

7. The citizens elect the senators. _____

8. Senators can be re-elected. _____

**F.   Circle the correct verb form in each sentence.**

1. Roosevelt ( remembers / is remembered ) for the New Deal.
2. Many soldiers ( killed / were killed ) in the Revolutionary War.
3. Congress ( signed / was signed ) the Declaration of Independence in 1776.
4. President's Day ( celebrates / is celebrated ) in February.
5. Soldiers ( march / are marched ) in Veterans Day parades.
6. Flags ( carry / are carried ) in the parade.
7. Native Americans ( taught / were taught ) the Pilgrims how to plant corn.
8. Native Americans ( invited / were invited ) to the first Thanksgiving.
9. The Pilgrims ( came / were come ) from Europe.
10. Dr. Martin Luther King Jr. ( fought / was fought ) for civil rights.

**G.   Match the two parts of each sentence.**

1. Soldiers who died in wars
2. Thanksgiving
3. Large turkey meals
4. The first Monday in September
5. The Fourth of July
6. The Declaration of Independence
7. The Liberty Bell
8. Dr. Martin Luther King Jr.
9. Dr. Martin Luther King Jr. Day

a. is celebrated with fireworks.
b. are remembered on Veterans Day.
c. was chosen as the date for Labor Day.
d. is found in Philadelphia.
e. is celebrated in November.
f. was assassinated in 1968.
g. was first celebrated in 1986.
h. are eaten on Thanksgiving.
i. was signed in Philadelphia.

**H.   Using the information given, write active and passive voice sentences.**

| police officers | issue | tickets |
|---|---|---|

1. (active) _The police officers issue tickets._

2. (passive) _Tickets are issued by police officers._

| teachers | make | classroom rules |
|---|---|---|

1. (active) _____

2. (passive) _____

| business owner | hire | employees |
|---|---|---|

1. (active) _____

2. (passive) _____

# LESSON **4** Community concerns

---

**GOAL** ■ Express opinions

**A.** **Read each situation and decide what you could do. Come up with two possible solutions.**

1. The class at school that you want to take is full. What could you do?

   Possibility: I could _____.

   Possibility: I could _____.

2. The person sitting next to you is always talking and you can't hear the teacher. What could you do?

   Possibility: I could _____.

   Possibility: I could _____.

3. There is so much traffic in the morning that you are always late to class. What could you do?

   Possibility: I could _____.

   Possibility: I could _____.

4. The people living next to you are always up late making a lot of noise. What could you do?

   Possibility: I could _____.

   Possibility: I could _____.

**B.** **Choose the best solution from each scenario and write *should* statements.**

1. I should _____.

2. _____

3. _____

4. _____

## C. Study the chart.

| Modal *Should* | | | | |
|---|---|---|---|---|
| **Subject** | **Modal** | **Base verb** | | |
| I<br>You<br>He<br>She<br>It<br>We<br>They | should | clean up<br>attend<br>be<br>raise | after your dog.<br>the community meetings.<br>home before midnight.<br>taxes to hire teachers. | We use the modal *should* to give advice or a strong suggestion. |

## D. Correct the mistake in each sentence below. If the sentence is correct, write *correct* on the line.

              be

1. There should ~~is~~ rent control in that neighborhood.    _____

2. The police officers shoulds ask for help.    _____

3. The neighbors should met to discuss the problems.    _____

4. The cars should is parked in the parking lot.    _____

5. The teachers should be on the playground at lunch time.    _____

6. The city council should setting a curfew for teenagers.    _____

7. We should start an organization to clean up the community.    _____

8. The lights should turned on at dusk.    _____

**E.** **Complete each sentence with *should* and a verb that makes sense.**

1. The police officers _____ the homeless people where the shelter is.

2. The city _____ more lights in the parks.

3. The school _____ sandbox.

4. The neighborhood _____ a neighborhood watch.

5. The car owners who park on the street _____ their doors at night.

6. The mayor _____ the firefighters who need more trucks.

**F.** **Come up with solutions for each problem. Use *should* in your solution.**

1. There are not enough sidewalks for children to walk to school.

   *The city should raise taxes to build more sidewalks.*

2. There is too much trash in the streets.

   _____

3. There has been an increase in crime.

   _____

4. There are not enough libraries in the community.

   _____

5. The city playground is too far away for many neighborhood children to visit.

   _____

6. A municipal swimming pool might give children a place to go in the summer.

   _____

7. It's dangerous for children to swim in the river under the bridge.

   _____

8. There is only one city policeman on patrol in the city at night.

   _____

# LESSON **5** If I were president

**GOAL** ■ Write a speech

**A.** **There are many ways to express your opinions. Look at the phrases below and use them to write your ideas about your school, your community, or your country.**

1. In my opinion, _____.

2. I believe that _____.

3. As I see it, _____.

4. Personally, I think _____.

5. I feel that _____.

6. I think that _____.

**B.** **Answer the questions below.**

1. If you won a million dollars, what would you do?

   _____

   _____

2. If you were a teacher, what would you teach?

   _____

   _____

3. If you could live in a different country, where would you live?

   _____

   Why? _____

4. If you could meet one famous person, who would it be?

   _____

   Why? _____

**C. Study the chart.**

| Contrary-to-Fact Conditionals | |
|---|---|
| **Possibility:** *if* + subject + past tense | **Possible result:** *would* + base form |
| **If** we **spent** more money on education, | we **would have** better schools. |
| **If** we **didn't have** a police force, | there **would be** more crime. |
| **Rules** <br> • Use contrary-to-fact conditionals to describe situations that aren't true now and that the speaker thinks will probably never be true. <br> • Use a comma after the *if* clause when it comes first. <br> • In formal English, use *were* for the past tense of *be* with all subjects in the *if* clause. | |

**D. Fill in each blank with the correct tense of the verb in parentheses.**

1. If housing prices (be) _____ *were* _____ lower, we (move) _____ *would move* _____ to a larger apartment.

2. If they (increase) _____ taxes, I (move) _____ away.

3. If they (build) _____ a new park, the children (have) _____ a better place to play.

4. If people (clean up) _____ after their dogs, the streets (look) _____ a lot better.

5. If prices (be) _____ more affordable, we (buy) _____ a house.

6. If we (have) _____ less traffic, there (be) _____ fewer accidents.

7. If the city (provide) _____ cheap housing, the community (be) _____ more diverse.

8. If the river (not be) _____ dirty, we (swim) _____ in it.

**E. Complete each sentence. Use the correct form of the verbs in the box.**

| have | feel | be | ~~give~~ |
|------|------|-----|------|
| like | improve | learn | work |

1. If I were mayor, I _____ *would give* _____ more money to the schools.

2. If schools _____ more money, students would have newer books.

3. If they had newer books, students _____ more interested in learning.

4. If they were more interested in learning, they _____ more.

5. If students learned more, they _____ their own intelligence.

6. If they _____ proud of themselves, they would also feel happier.

7. If students were happier, they _____ school more.

8. If they liked school more, they _____ harder.

**F. Using the answers you wrote to the questions in Exercise B, write complete sentences using contrary-to-fact conditionals.**

**EXAMPLE:** If I won a million dollars, I would pay for my children's college education.

1. _____

_____

2. _____

_____

3. _____

_____

4. _____

_____

# PRACTICE TEST

## A. Read and choose the best answer.

> If you vote for me as mayor, I will clean up our parks and build more libraries; I will help small businesses by lowering business taxes and keeping the minimum wage the same; I will work with local hospitals and clinics to improve the efficiency of their healthcare; I will not raise your local taxes; I will not spend government money on personal vacations; and I will not allow crime to take over our city. I will work hard and do right by our city.

1. What is the candidate running for?
   a. senator
   b. police chief
   c. city manager
   d. mayor

2. How will the candidate help small businesses?
   a. by raising the minimum wage
   b. by raising local taxes
   c. by lowering business taxes
   d. by lowering minimum wage

3. What will the candidate NOT do?
   a. raise taxes
   b. allow crime to increase
   c. use government money for vacations
   d. a, b, and c

4. How will the candidate help the healthcare system?
   a. by building more hospitals
   b. by hiring more doctors
   c. by putting medical records online
   d. none of the above

5. What does the candidate plan to do?
   a. clean up the libraries
   b. plan vacations
   c. build more parks
   d. clean up the parks

# GLOSSARY OF GRAMMAR TERMS

| | |
|---|---|
| **adjective** | a word that describes a noun (Example: the _red_ hat) |
| **adverb** | a word that modifies a verb, adjective, or another adverb (Example: She eats _quickly_.) |
| **affirmative** | not negative and not a question (Example: _I like him._) |
| **apostrophe** | a punctuation mark that shows missing letters in contractions or possession (Example: _It's_ or _Jim's_) |
| **article** | words used before a noun (Example: _a_, _an_, _the_) |
| **base form** | the main form of a verb, used without _to_ (Example: _be_, _have_, _study_) |
| **comma** | a punctuation mark used to indicate a pause or separation (Example: I live in an apartment_,_ and you live in a house.) |
| **complement** | a word or words that add to or complete an idea after the verb (Example: He is _happy_.) |
| **conjugation** | the form of a verb (Example: I _am_, You _are_, We _are_, They _are_, He _is_, She _is_, It _is_) |
| **continuous form** | a verb form that expresses action during time (Example: He _is shopping_.) |
| **contraction** | shortening of a word, syllable, or word group by omission of a sound or letter (Example: It is = _It's_, does not = _doesn't_) |
| **count nouns** | nouns that can be counted by number (Example: one _apple_, two _apples_) |
| **definite article** | use of _the_ when a noun is known to speaker and listener (Example: I know _the_ store.) |
| **exclamation mark** | a punctuation symbol marking surprise or emotion (Example: Hello_!_) |
| **formal** | polite or respectful language (Example: _Could_ you _please_ give me that?) |
| **imperative** | a command form of a verb (Example: _Listen_! or _Look out_!) |
| **indefinite article** | _a_ or _an_ used before a noun when something is talked about for the first time or when _the_ is too specific (Example: There's _a_ new restaurant.) |
| **infinitive** | the main form of a verb, usually used with _to_ (Example: I like _to run_ fast.) |
| **informal** | friendly or casual language (Example: _Can_ I have that?) |
| **irregular verb** | a verb different from regular form verbs (Example: be = _am, are, is, was, were, being_) |
| **modal auxiliary** | a verb that indicates a mood (ability, possibility, etc.) and is followed by the base form of another verb (Example: I _can read_ English well.) |
| **modifier** | a word phrase that describes another (Example: a _good_ friend) |
| **negative** | the opposite of affirmative (Example: She _does not_ like meat.) |
| **noun** | a name of a person, place, or thing (Example: _Joe_, _England_, _bottle_) |
| **noncount nouns** | nouns impossible or difficult to count (Example: _water_, _love_, _rice_, _fire_) |

| | |
|---|---|
| **object, direct** | the focus of a verb's action (Example: I eat _oranges_.) |
| **object pronoun** | replaces the noun taking the action (Example: _Julia_ is nice. I like _her_.) |
| **past tense** | a verb form used to express an action or state in the past (Example: You _worked_ yesterday.) |
| **period** | a punctuation mark ending a sentence (.) |
| **plural** | indicating more than one (Example: _pencils_, _children_) |
| **possessive adjective** | an adjective expressing possession (Example: _our_ car) |
| **preposition** | a word that indicates relationship between objects (Example: _on_ the _desk_) |
| **present tense** | a verb tense representing the current time, not past or future (Example: They _are_ at home right now.) |
| **pronoun** | a word used in place of a noun (Example: _Ted_ is 65. _He_ is retired.) |
| **question form** | to ask or look for an answer (Example: _Where is my book?_) |
| **regular verb** | verb with endings that are regular and follow the rule (Example: work = _work_, _works_, _worked_, _working_) |
| **sentence** | a thought expressed in words, with a subject and verb (Example: _Julia works hard_.) |
| **short answer** | a response to a _yes/no_ question, usually a subject pronoun and auxiliary verb (Example: _Yes, I am_, or _No, he doesn't_.) |
| **singular** | one object (Example: _a cat_) |
| **statement** | a sentence or thought (Example: _The weather is rainy today_.) |
| **subject** | the noun that does the action in a sentence (Example: _The gardener works_ here.) |
| **subject pronoun** | a pronoun that takes the place of a subject (Example: _John_ is a sudent. _He_ is smart.) |
| **syllable** | a part of a word as determined by vowel sounds and rhythm (Example: _ta-ble_) |
| **tag questions** | short informal questions that come at the end of sentences in speech (Example: You like soup, _don't you?_ They aren't hungry, _are they?_) |
| **tense** | the part of a verb that shows the past, present, or future time (Example: He _talked_.) |
| **verb** | word describing an action or state (Example: The boys _walk_ to school. I _am_ tired.) |
| **vowels** | the letters _a, e, i o, u,_ and sometimes _y_ |
| **_wh-_ questions** | questions that ask for information, usually starting with _Who, What, When, Where,_ or _Why_. (Example: _Where_ do you live?) _How_ is often included in this group. |
| **_yes/no_ questions** | questions that ask for an affirmative or a negative answer (Example: _Are you happy?_) |

# GRAMMAR REFERENCE

| Present Tense | | |
|---|---|---|
| **Subject** | **Present tense** | |
| I | send | memos. |
| You | take | orders from customers. |
| The custodian | clean**s** | the bathrooms. |
| We | deliver | packages. |
| They | fix | leaky pipes. |

**Rules**
- Use the present tense to describe what someone does at his or her job.
- For sentences with *he, she,* or *it,* use *-s* or *-es* at the end of the verb.

| Present Tense *Yes/No* Questions and Answers | | | | |
|---|---|---|---|---|
| *Do/Does* | **Subject** | **Base verb** | | **Answer** |
| Do | I<br>you<br>we<br>they | have | a pool?<br>four bedrooms?<br>air conditioning? | Yes, I do.<br>No, you don't.<br>Yes, we do.<br>No, they don't. |
| Does | he<br>she | want | a bigger place?<br>a yard for her dog? | Yes, he does.<br>No, she doesn't. |

| Past Tense (Regular Verbs) | | | | |
|---|---|---|---|---|
| **Subject** | **Rule** | **Past tense verbs** | | |
| I, You, We, They<br>He, She, It | base verb + *-ed* | work**ed** | start**ed** | want**ed** |
| | | finish**ed** | help**ed** | attend**ed** |
| | base verb + *-d* | liv**ed** | lik**ed** | |
| | | hop**ed** | complet**ed** | |
| | base verb *-y* + *-ied* | stud**ied** | hurr**ied** | marr**ied** |
| | | worr**ied** | carr**ied** | |

| Past Tense (Irregular Verbs) | | |
|---|---|---|
| **Subject** | **Base form** | **Irregular form** |
| I, You, We, They<br>He, She, It | go | **went** |
| | take | **took** |
| | come | **came** |
| | have | **had** |
| | become | **became** |

| Past Tense (*To be*) | |
|---|---|
| **Subject** | *To be* |
| I | **was** |
| You, We, They | **were** |
| He, She, It | **was** |

*base verb = the pure verb form (to work: <u>work</u> = base verb; to start: <u>start</u> = base verb)

| Future Time Clauses with *When* | | |
|---|---|---|
| **Sequence of events** | **happens first** | **happens second** |
| | **Time clause (Simple present)** | **Independent clause (Future tense with *will*)** |
| | When they *apply* to college, | they *will look* for scholarships. |
| | When the girls *go* to school, | they *will get* part-time jobs. |
| | When he *has* extra money, | Lam *will send* it to the girls. |
| **Note:** The order of the clauses does not matter. *When they apply to college, they will look for scholarships* and *They will look for scholarships when they apply to college* have the same meaning. | | |

| Adverbial Time Clauses with Future Meaning | |
|---|---|
| **Main clause** | **Time clause** |
| I'll review for the test | **before** I go to class tomorrow. |
| Gloria will take a shower | **after** she gets home. |
| My children will take piano lessons | **when** they are ready. |
| They won't study | **until** I tell them to. |
| **Rules** | |
| • Use the future tense in the main clause and the simple present in the time clause. | |
| • *Until* means "up to that time." | |

| Time Clauses with *When* | | | |
|---|---|---|---|
| **Time** | **Main clause** | ***When* clause** | **Verb tense** |
| **Past** | My brother **got** his first job | when he **was** 17 years old. | **past** |
| **Present** | I always **do** my homework | when I **get** home from my job. | **present** |
| **Future** | She **will get** a full-time job | when her kids **go** to college. | **future, present** |
| **Note:** If the *when* clause comes before the main clause, use a comma (,). | | | |

## Be + Infinitive

| Subject | Verb (*to be*) | Infinitive | | Rule |
|---|---|---|---|---|
| My goal | **is** | **to get** | a job. | The infinitive comes after *be* to express future actions or events such as <u>hope</u>, a <u>dream</u>, or a <u>goal</u>. |
| One solution | **is** | **to work** | part time. | |
| Another solution | **is** | **to have** | my mother help. | |
| My dream | **is** | **to own** | my own business. | |

## Be + Gerund

| Subject | Verb (*to be*) | Gerund | | Rule |
|---|---|---|---|---|
| A good study habit | **is** | **asking** | questions in class. | The gerund comes after *be* to express results, solutions, secrets, keys, or activities. |
| A bad study habit | **is** | **copying** | your friend's homework. | |
| My secret | **is** | **studying** | in a quiet place. | |
| My best study habit | **is** | **rewriting** | my class notes. | |

## Gerunds after Prepositions

| Subject | Verb | Adjective | Preposition | Gerund / Noun | |
|---|---|---|---|---|---|
| I | am | happy | about | **getting** | a new job. |
| She | is | good | at | **fixing** | machines. |
| They | are | interested | in | **computers.** | |
| He | is | afraid | of | **not having** | enough experience. |

**Rules**
- A gerund or a noun follows an adjective + preposition.
  Other examples of adjective + preposition are *tired of, bad at,* and *worried about.*
- To make the gerund negative, put *not* before the gerund.

## Gerunds and Infinitives

| Subject | Main verb | Infinitive or gerund | | Verb rule | Other verbs that follow the same rule |
|---|---|---|---|---|---|
| He | wants | **to get** | a job. | *Want* is followed by an infinitive (*to* + verb). | plan, decide, agree, hope, learn, promise |
| She | enjoys | **fixing** | bicycles. | *Enjoy* is followed by a gerund (verb + *-ing*). | finish, give up, recommend, suggest |
| They | like | **walking. to walk.** | | *Like* is followed by a gerund or an infinitive. | love, hate, begin, continue, start |

| Superlative Adjectives | | | |
|---|---|---|---|
| **Type of adjective** | **Adjective** | **Superlative** | **Rule** |
| Short (1–2 syllables) | small<br>slow | the smallest<br>the slowest | add *-est* |
| Long (3+ syllables) | beautiful | the most beautiful | add *the most* before the adjective |
| Adjectives that end in *-e* | large<br>safe | the largest<br>the safest | add *-st* |
| Adjectives that end in *–y* | pretty<br>easy | the prettiest<br>the easiest | change the *-y* to *-i* and add *-est* |
| Adjectives that end in consonant-vowel-consonant | big<br>hot<br>flat | the biggest<br>the hottest<br>the flattest | double the final consonant and add *-est* |
| Irregular | good<br>bad | the best<br>the worst | These adjectives are irregular. |

**Note:** Always use *the* before a superlative.

| Comparative Adjectives | | | |
|---|---|---|---|
| **Type of adjective** | **Adjective** | **Comparative** | **Rule** |
| Short (1–2 syllables) | small<br>slow | smaller<br>slower | add *-er* |
| Long (3+ syllables) | beautiful | more beautiful | add *more* before the adjective |
| Adjectives that end in *-e* | large<br>safe | larger<br>safer | add *-r* |
| Adjectives that end in *-y* | pretty<br>easy | prettier<br>easier | change the *-y* to *-i* and add *-er* |
| Adjectives that end in consonant-vowel-consonant | big<br>hot<br>flat | bigger<br>hotter<br>flatter | double the final consonant and add *-er* |
| Irregular | good<br>bad | better<br>worse | These adjectives are irregular. |

## Comparative and Superlative Questions

| Question word | Subject | Verb | Adjective or Noun | Rule |
|---|---|---|---|---|
| Which | one<br>place<br>store<br>Ø | is | bigger?<br>closer to the bus stop?<br>the best? | Use *be* before an adjective. |
| | | has | more shoes?<br>the fewest employees? | Use *have* before a noun. |

## Answers

| Question | Short answer | Long answer | Rules |
|---|---|---|---|
| Which store is bigger, the shoe store or the clothing store? | The clothing store. | The clothing store *is bigger*. | • When talking about two things and mentioning both of them, use *than*. |
| | | The clothing store *is bigger than* the shoe store. | |
| Which one has more employees? | The shoe store. | The shoe store *has more employees*. | • When talking about two things but only mentioning one of them, **do not** use *than*. |
| | | The shoe store *has more employees than* the clothing store. | |

## Comparatives and Superlatives with Nouns

| Comparatives using nouns | Explanation |
|---|---|
| The apartment has **more bedrooms** than the condo. | Use *more* or *fewer* to compare count nouns. |
| The condo has **fewer bedrooms** than the apartment. | |
| The condo gets **more sun** than the apartment. | Use *more* or *less* to compare noncount nouns. |
| The apartment gets **less light** than the condo. | |
| The condo has **the most bathrooms**. | Use *the most* or *the fewest* for count nouns. |
| The apartment has **the fewest appliances**. | |
| The condo has **the most space** outdoors. | Use *the most* or *the least* for noncount nouns. |
| The apartment has **the least space** outdoors. | |

## Past Continuous

| Subject | *Be* (past) | Verb + *-ing* | | Explanation |
|---|---|---|---|---|
| I | **was** | **working** | on my budget. | The past continuous describes what was in progress at a specific moment in the past. |
| Vu | **was** | **writing** | everything down. | |
| Maryanne | **was** | **trying** | to help. | |
| They | **were** | **worrying** | about their phone bill. | |

## Past Continuous with *While*

| Short action | *While* | Long action | Short action |
|---|---|---|---|
| The phone rang | **while** | she was studying. | |
| I saw a mouse | | I was cleaning. | |
| The oven broke | | they were cooking. | |
| | **While** | she was studying, | the phone rang. |
| | | I was cleaning, | I saw a mouse. |
| | | they were cooking, | the oven broke. |

### Rules
- Use the *past continuous* to talk about things that started in the past and continued for a period of time.
- Use the *simple past* to talk about a short action that happened once.
- To connect two events that happened in the past, use the past continuous with *while* for the longer event. Use the simple past for the shorter event.
- **Note:** You can reverse the two clauses, but you need a comma if *while* comes first.

## Time Clauses with *When* and *While*

| *When* | Short action | *While* | Long action | Short action |
|---|---|---|---|---|
| | The phone rang | **while** | she was studying. | |
| | | **While** | she was studying, | the phone rang. |
| **When** | the phone rang, | | she was studying. | |

### Rules
- Use *while* + the past continuous with a long continuous action.
- Use *when* + the simple past with a short non-continuous action.
- If the time clause (the clause with *while* or *when*) comes before the main clause, use a comma.

## Present Perfect

| Subject | *Have* | Past participle | | Period of time | Example sentence |
|---|---|---|---|---|---|
| I, You, We, They | **have** | **been** | sick | since Tuesday | I *have been* sick since Tuesday. |
| She, He, It | **has** | **had** | a backache | for two weeks | She *has had* a backache for two weeks. |

### Rule
Use the present perfect for events starting in the past and continuing up to the present.

## Present Perfect Questions

| Have | Subject | Past participle | | Period of time | Example question |
|------|---------|-----------------|------|----------------|------------------|
| **Have** | I, you, we, they | **been** | sick | since Tuesday? | *Have* you *been* sick since Tuesday? |
| **Has** | she, he, it | **had** | a backache | for two weeks? | *Has* she *had* a backache for two weeks? |

## Meanings of the Present Perfect

| Example | Explanation |
|---------|-------------|
| He **has worked** here for ten years. | an action that continues from the past to the present |
| I **have seen** the doctor twice this month. | a repeated past action that is completed |
| They **have lived** in France. | a past action that does not mention a specific time |

**Rules**
- The present perfect has three different meanings.
- The contractions *'s* and *'ve* can be used in affirmative sentences.
    He**'s** worked here for ten years. They**'ve** lived in France.
- The contractions *hasn't* and *haven't* can be used in negative statements.
    I **haven't** talked with Dr. Perkins. He **hasn't** examined me.

## *For* and *Since*

| Present perfect statement | Time expression |
|---------------------------|-----------------|
| I have gone to Dr. Jenks | **for** ten years. |
| She has been in the same office | **since** 2003. |
| Ali has not had a cold | **for** several years. |
| We have not taken any medicine | **since** Monday. |

**Rules**
- Use *for* when an action has continued for a certain amount of time.
- Use *since* when an action began at a specific time.

## Adverbial Clauses with *Because* and *So (that)*

| Main clause | *because / so (that)* | Adverbial clause |
|-------------|------------------------|------------------|
| Zhou went to night school | **because** | he needed a better degree for his job. |
| His boss won't promote him | **because** | he doesn't have a college degree. |
| Zhou's mother is coming | **so (that)** | she can take care of the twins. |
| They are looking for a bigger house | **so (that)** | they will have room for everyone. |

**Note:** Adverbial clauses with *because* give reasons <u>why</u>. Clauses with *so* or *so that* give <u>purposes</u>.

## Causative with *Get*

| Subject | *Get* | Object | Past participle | | Explanation |
|---|---|---|---|---|---|
| I | **get** | my car | washed | every Sunday. | Causative means that the subject causes something to happen. |
| We | **got** | our picture | taken. | | |
| They | **will get** | the roof | fixed | next year. | Any tense of the verb *get* can be used. |

## Present Perfect Continuous

| Subject | *Have/Has* | *Been* | Present participle | |
|---|---|---|---|---|
| I | **have** | **been** | **working** | here for six months. |
| She | **has** | **been** | **receiving** | benefits since May. |
| You | **have** | **been** | **doing** | a good job. |

**Rules**

- The present perfect and the present perfect continuous mean almost the same thing.
- If the action is happening at this very minute, it is better to use the present perfect continuous, *not* the present perfect: I *have been waiting* for you since noon. **Not** *I have waited* for you since noon.
- Do not use the continuous form with non-action verbs such as *like, love, have, want, know, own, hear, see, seem,* and *understand.*

## Future Conditional

| Cause | Effect |
|---|---|
| *If* + present tense | Future tense |
| **If** you **smoke,** | you **will get** lung cancer. |
| **If** they **don't exercise,** | they **will gain** weight. |
| **If** we **don't get** enough sleep, | we **will be** tired. |
| **If** I **run** every day, | I **will stay** in shape. |
| **If** he **doesn't eat** enough calcium, | he **won't have** strong bones. |

**Rules**
- Use a future conditional statement to connect a cause and an effect.
- The *if*-clause (or the *cause*) is in the present tense and the *effect* clause is in the future tense.
- You can reverse the clauses, but use a comma only when the *if*-clause comes first.
   I will stay in shape *if* I run every day.
   *If* I run every day, I will stay in shape.

## Contrary-to-Fact Conditionals

| Possibility: *if* + subject + past tense | Possible result: *would* + base form |
|---|---|
| **If** we **spent** more money on education, | we **would have** better schools. |
| **If** we **didn't have** a police force, | there **would be** more crime. |

**Rules**
- Use contrary-to-fact conditionals to describe situations that aren't true now and that the speaker thinks will probably never be true.
- Use a comma after the *if* clause when it comes first.
- In formal English, use *were* for the past tense of *be* with all subjects in the *if* clause.

## Adverbial Time Clauses in the Past Tense

| Main clause | Time clause | Meaning |
|---|---|---|
| She took a shower | **after** she woke up. | First, she woke up. Second, she took a shower. |
| He went to the bank | **before** he stopped by the dry cleaners. | First, he went to the bank. Second, he stopped by the dry cleaners. |
| She was tired | **when** she got home. | She got home and was tired at the *same time*. |

**Explanation**
- The time clause can go before or after the main clause.
- Use a comma after the time clause when it comes at the beginning of the sentence.
  After she woke up, she took a shower. / She took a shower after she woke up.

  Before she went to the bookstore, she stopped at the bank. / She stopped at the bank before she went to the bookstore.

## Statements of Necessity

| Subject | Modal | Base Verb | | Explanation |
|---|---|---|---|---|
| Jared | **has to** | go | to the bank. | |
| We | **have to** | meet | at the restaurant at 5 p.m. | *Must* and *have to* show necessity. |
| Jared | **must** | finish | his English essay before class on Tuesday. | |
| They | **must** | help | their parents move tomorrow. | |

## Modal: *Should*

| Subject | Modal | Base verb | | Explanation |
|---|---|---|---|---|
| I<br>You<br>He<br>She<br>It<br>We<br>They | **should** | clean<br>attend<br>be<br>raise | the bedroom.<br>the community meetings.<br>home before midnight.<br>taxes to hire teachers. | We use the modal *should* to give advice or a strong suggestion. |

## Modals: *Could/Might*

| Subject | Modal | Base Verb | | Explanation |
|---|---|---|---|---|
| I<br>You<br>He<br>She<br>It<br>We<br>They | **could** | fall<br>get<br>lose | off the ladder.<br>hurt.<br>a lot of money. | We use the modals *might* and *could* to say that there is a chance that something will happen in the future. |
| | **might** | miss | work. | |

## *Used to*

| Example | Explanation |
|---|---|
| I *used to* **work** for Data Computers. | *Used to* + base form describes a repeated action in the past or a situation that existed in the past. |
| I *am used to* **working** with computers. | *Be used to* + gerund describes an action or a situation that has become familiar. |

## *Would rather*

| | *Would* | Subject | *Rather* | Base form | *Or* | Base form |
|---|---|---|---|---|---|---|
| Questions | **Would** | Kim | **rather** | type | or | answer phones? |
| | **Would** | You | **rather** | work days | or | (work) nights? |

| | Subject | *Would rather* | Base form | *Than* | Base form |
|---|---|---|---|---|---|
| Statements | She | **would rather** | answer phones | than | type. |
| | I | **'d rather** | work days | than | nights. |

**Rules**
- *Or* is used between the choices in a question.
- *Than* is used between the choices in a statement.
- The second verb in questions and statements can be omitted if it is the same as the first.
- *Would* is often contracted in statements: **I'd, you'd, he'd, she'd, we'd, they'd.**

## *Prefer . . . to*

| Subject | *Prefer* | Noun | *to* | Noun |
|---|---|---|---|---|
| I | **prefer** | health benefits | **to** | dental benefits. |
| She | **prefers** | day care | **to** | overtime. |
| He | **prefers** | working | **to** | studying. |
| They | **prefer** | paid vacation | **to** | paid personal days. |

**Rules**
- Use *prefer* to give your preferences.
- Use *to* between the two nouns

## Reported Speech

| Subject | Verb | Object | Infinitive | |
|---------|------|--------|------------|---|
| I | asked | her | to finish | the report. |
| She | told | me | to work<br>not to be | faster.<br>so slow. |

| Subject | Verb | Object | Preposition | Gerund/Noun |
|---------|------|--------|-------------|-------------|
| I | thanked | her | for | helping me.<br>not being angry. |
| They | criticized | me | for | leaving early.<br>not staying late. |
| We | praised | him | for | his management skills. |

## Reported Speech

| Direct Speech | Reported Speech |
|---------------|-----------------|
| Marco asked, "How *are* **you** feeling?" | Marco asked how **I** *was feeling*. |
| Eli said, "**I** *want* to tell **you** a story." | Eli said **he** *wanted* to tell **me** a story. |
| Eli said, "**I** *went* to the city council meeting yesterday." | Eli said **he** *had gone* to the city council meeting yesterday. |
| The mayor promised, "**I** *will spend* more money on schools." | The mayor promised **he** *would spend* more money on schools. |

**Rules**
- In reported speech, the verb tenses change to the past of the direct speech form.
  - simple present ⟶ simple past
  - present continuous ⟶ past continuous
  - simple past ⟶ past perfect
  - modal *will* ⟶ modal *would*
- The subject pronouns change.
- Quotation marks are not used and there is no comma after *said, asked, promised,* etc.

## Active and Passive Voice

| Active Voice | Passive Voice (*be* + past participle) |
|--------------|----------------------------------------|
| The city clerk **issues** marriage licenses. | Marriage licenses **are issued by** the city clerk. |
| The city council member **represents** the citizens. | The citizens **are represented by** the city council member |

**Rules**
- The active voice shows that the subject of the sentence performs the action.
- The passive voice shows that the subject of the sentence receives the action.
- *Be* in a passive sentence is in the same tense as the verb in the active sentence.

| Polite Requests: *Would you mind . . .* and *Could you . . . ?* | |
|---|---|
| **Request** | **Description** |
| **Would you mind** making a copy for me? | polite and formal |
| **Could you look** over this report? | polite and less formal |
| **Can you help** me with this box? | polite and informal |
| Give me that! | very informal or impolite |

**Rules**
- *Would you mind* is followed by a gerund.
- *Can* and *could* are followed by the base form.
- Use polite and formal language when talking with a boss or manager.
- Use polite or informal language when talking with coworkers.
- Use very informal or impolite language in an emergency or to show anger.

| *But* and *However* | | |
|---|---|---|
| **First idea** | **Second idea** | **Statement of contrast** |
| California is on the West Coast. | New Jersey isn't on the West Coast. | California is on the West Coast, **but** New Jersey isn't. |
| Texas produces a lot of oil. | Kentucky doesn't produce a lot of oil. | Texas produces a lot of oil; **however,** Kentucky doesn't. |

**Rules**
- Use a comma before a contrasting statement that starts with *but*.
- Use a semicolon before a contrasting statement that starts with *however* and use a comma after the word *however*.
- Use the subject and a helping verb in the contrasting statement.
  California is on the West Coast, but New Jersey isn't ~~on the West Coast~~.
  Texas produces a lot of oil; however, Kentucky doesn't ~~produce a lot of oil~~.

| *Both* and *Neither* | | |
|---|---|---|
| **First idea** | **Second idea** | **Statement of agreement** |
| Enrico wants to lower class sizes in elementary schools. | Ali wants to lower class sizes in elementary schools. | **Both** Enrico **and** Ali want to lower class sizes in elementary schools. |
| Enrico doesn't want high taxes. | Ali doesn't want high taxes. | **Neither** Enrico **nor** Ali wants high taxes. |

**Rules**
- Use *and* in statements beginning with *both*.
- Use *nor* in statements beginning with *neither*.
- In a *both/and* statement, the verb agrees with the combined subject.
  *Both* Maria *and* Marco **are** citizens.
- In a *neither/nor* statement, the verb agrees with the second subject.
  *Neither* Maria *nor* Marco **is** a citizen.

| Imperatives | | | |
|---|---|---|---|
| **Negative** | **Base verb** | | **Rules** |
| Do not | waste | time. | • Use the imperative to give instructions or commands.<br>• The subject of the imperative is *you*, but don't include it in the statement. |
| | Keep | a schedule. | |
| | Wake up | early. | |
| Don't | forget | your schedule. | |

| Transition Words | | |
|---|---|---|
| **Numbers** | **Without numbers** | **Rules** |
| First, (First of all,) | First, | • Do not use numbers as transition words if there are more than four steps.<br>• When not using numbers, *next, then,* and *after that* can be used in any order to describe more than one step.<br>• Always finish with the words *finally* or *lastly*. |
| Second, | Next, | |
| Third, | Then, | |
| | After that, | |
| Finally, (Lastly,) | Finally, | |

| Editing | | |
|---|---|---|
| **Mechanic** | **Rule** | **Examples** |
| Capital letters | Every proper noun should begin with a capital letter. | <u>S</u>he loves her hometown.<br><u>G</u>loria lives in <u>V</u>ictoria. |
| Nouns | Every noun should be in the correct singular or plural form. | He has **a** good **job**. (not *jobs*)<br>They have five **children**. (not *childrens*) |
| Verbs | Every verb should be in the correct tense and agree with the noun. | Our family **can buy** a nice house.<br>There **are** three parks. |
| Punctuation | Every sentence should end with a period, question mark, or exclamation point. | Gloria never wants to move<u>.</u><br>Where do you live<u>?</u> |

# PHOTO CREDITS

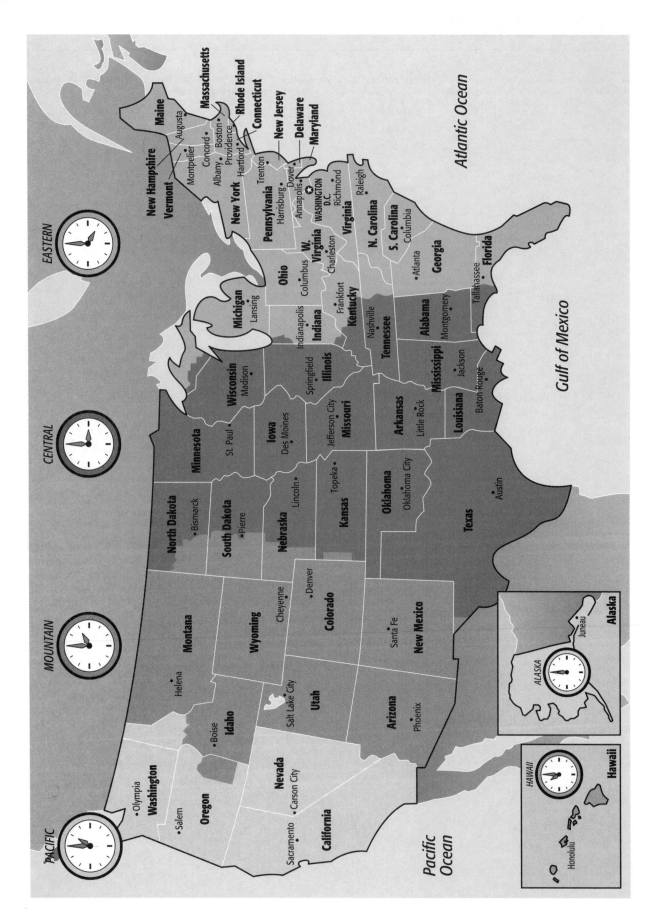